# IN THE TIME OF THE INFORMATION TECHNOLOGY FEEDING FRENZY

## Don Felice

### Guidelines of America

# TABLE OF CONTENTS

# INTRODUCTION

If you had anything, anything at all, to do with Information Technology during that period (*the eighties and early nineties*), you know what an exciting period it was! New products were coming into the Market from every direction! They weren't all good - or useful - or even practical. But they were NEW! New ideas were being tried out. They were being bought, sold, trampled down, bartered, laughed at, scorned, or envied.

New sales techniques and gimmicks were being tested. It was an absolute feeding frenzy! Throw a new product into the market and watch what happens! Maybe nothing, but usually it caused a great commotion - which might not last all that long because another new product had just been thrown in and attention was diverted.

Think about it! At the 1989 Fall COMDEX there was **one** product that stole the whole show. The POQUET Pocket Computer was introduced. 200,000 people wanted to see it, touch it, and marvel over it. For days, the lines to get up to the counter at that booth were four or five deep. The little machines were chained to the counter with a chain that weighed more than the computer! There were no riots. The people were at least semi-polite. It just **looked** like a riot!

The booth was doing terrific business! POQUET computers were being sold by the thousand! Right? No, **wrong**! People wanted to see them and touch them. They didn't want to **buy** them! By the next year, the POQUET was a has-been. There was a booth on the show floor, but **nobody** stopped at it.

All the R&D money, all the Marketing money, and all the hopes and dreams of the developers evaporated. They had produced sizzle, but no steak, glitter, but no gold. That is **not** the path to success.

The "Big Fish" were gobbling up the little fish. Sometimes they wanted the little fish's product to be in their own product line. Sometimes they just wanted the new technology and not the product itself. Sometimes they wanted to prevent their competition from getting that new technology. Whatever the reason, they were making some very happy little fishes! Sometimes a little fish became an instant millionaire!

It was the time of the "User Group" and the "Conference." Any day of the year there was an I/T conference or User Group being held somewhere in the world. Frequently, there were many different conferences being held on the same day. Putting on I/T conferences had become a big business in its own right! Conferences on every imaginable I/T topic or sub-topic were being offered for the edification of the buying public. They were held in pleasant places, free gifts were offered, and, just being away from the office and on your company's expense account was a treat that was hard to refuse!

Establishing a User Group was a great idea! The company got to invite all its customers to come to one place at one time so they could be sold even more of the company's products. Come to your very own User Group, (*said the spider to the fly*) and see all our great new products - "you don't have to buy, just look."

Some smart companies realized that the things they had been doing have gotten them to where they are, but to go further, they had to do something **different**.

Perhaps there are areas they had not yet considered. What else can they do? Read through this material and then decide what more they could have done. I have suggested various areas that are frequently overlooked. They may not all work for every company, but if only one, two, or three of them do, it could make a significant difference in the bottom line and long-term success of any company.

I have attended, reported on, analyzed, and critiqued over four hundred I/T-related conferences. (*I was the Founder and principal writer for The CONFERENCE ANALYSIS NEWSLETTER.*) Nobody could attend that many conferences without learning a lot about how I/T-Ware was being sold. I have seen successes and failures. This book looks into the need for Salability as well as Sell Ability, the need for keeping your eye on your competition, the need for security, the need for support services, and the do's and don'ts of:

- User Groups
- Small Enticing Conferences
- Small Rewarding Conferences
- Small Deluding Conferences
- Mid-Sized Conferences
- International Conferences
- Really Big Conferences
- The Internet
- Electronic Commerce

If you think that is a lot to consider, you are right! Think of the poor Marketing Manager who had to decide so many different things: take into consideration everything on that list, plus: which conferences to buy a booth at? How big should it be? Who should man it? What products should be shown?

And then came the really hard decisions: What should the free giveaways be? Hats? T-Shirts? Water bottles? Or, the ever popular, pocket screwdrivers?

No wonder that guy gets the Big Bucks!

# SALABILITY

In order to sell well, a product — any product, I/T or not — must have intrinsic salability. That is, the prospective customer must need it or want it. Or, you must be able to **create** the need/want.

In order to cash in on the feeding frenzy, you still have to use the right bait.

Example: What have we always been told is the key to success? "Build a better mousetrap!" So, let us design (*virtually*) a "better mousetrap." When we are through, even technology-buffs who have no need for a mousetrap may want one of these! Our mousetrap should efficiently and effectively attract the little critters, cause them to no longer live (*notice how cleverly I avoided the word "kill"*), and dispose of their tiny carcasses without mess, fuss, or bother. (*The literature will have to emphasize that returning them to the wild after capture is no true solution because not only are they likely to return to your home, but they will continue to reproduce and reproduce and reproduce. So, our product not only provides a solution to **your** problem, but it provides a service to all mankind!*)

On to the product: We will attract the lusty beasts with the heady scent of pheromones. While still in a state of ecstasy, we will slip them a gaseous Mickey. While they dream of pleasures known only to mice, we will transport and transform them into a state of non-living. Then, we will cremate the carcass and deposit the ashes into a small, easily disposable plastic bag — or, if the product is to be used outdoors, a special feature should be available that will blow the ashes right out of our "better mouse trap." With that special feature we will be automatically providing fertilizer for the lawn, garden, farm, whatever. (*We have built an environmentally friendly mouse trap!*)

There you have it! Ease of use, ease of conscience (*no struggling little fuzz-ball with one leg caught in a trap*), efficiency, and no mess to clean up. We can offer a self-contained system that attracts, eliminates, and disposes of small rodent pests. Hey! We could build a larger version, get the appropriate pheromones, and significantly reduce the rat population worldwide (*while making a tidy profit!*).

Does our product have salability? Not yet. Need/Want is necessary, but not sufficient. In many (*most*) cases, other factors are extremely important, too. What you will find is that as you satisfy one factor, another suddenly pops up and urgently needs your attention. Price is an obvious and **major** factor (*always!*). If a product is way over priced, it won't sell! (*Except, maybe, in the Neiman Marcus Christmas catalog.*) If it is under priced and you don't make a profit, what's the point?

Another factor is the learning curve involved. (*Have you noticed that many new products come with no manual at all? Why do companies think that by eliminating the manual the customer will be faked into thinking that no manual is necessary? What do they provide in place of the good old-fashioned manual? On-line help — which is much cheaper to provide than is a hard-copy book. Most On-line help is no help at all! There may be lots of words, but they never answer the question you have. Please, charge me an extra two bucks and give me a **useful** manual!*) Customers want ease-of-learning and ease-of-use. That is why we have GUI. UNIX may be hot stuff for propeller heads, but it won't fly for the average Joe or Jill who wants off-the-shelf solutions and could not care less if they are written in UNIX, JOVIAL, JAVA, Sanskrit, Latin, or some Microsoft gobbledygook! Programmers (*now erroneously called "Software Engineers"*) don't mind the tough stuff. To them, it's "a challenge!" However, they are a special breed. They dwell in small cubicles or large garages. For the average Joes & Jills of this world, their mantra is "point and click."

Timing may also be a factor in salability. It doesn't always apply, but it should always be considered. For instance, our virtual mousetrap may sell better in the Fall when field mice begin to move indoors.

Is that everything? No! Or, at least, not necessarily. Depending on the product, there may be other factors. Example: Cosmetic appeal. *(Those bright-colored Apple machines may be a deciding factor to some buyers.)* Size could be a factor (*small footprint*). For Laptops there is weight to consider. Other factors could be capacity, speed, battery life, etc., etc. etc. Consider **everything**!

Oh yes! One of the other things to consider (*very seriously*) is competition. (!)

Realize that all the factors that affect salability need not be rational. Way back in the fifties, automobiles had to have fins or they didn't sell. The fins were useless, but they were necessary to make a sale. A few years ago, cup holders in cars became fashionable. Is the public's taste fickle? You bet! Should you be aware of what is popular and what is coming down the pike? You bet!

What is involved with determining salability is a combination of art and science. Don't ignore either one!

How do you know when a product is salable? Test it! Ask yourself, is it useful? Is it usable? Test it **AS A USER**. Don't just look for bugs. See if you can comfortably use the product. If you **can't** use it or don't **like** using it, how are you going to sell it?

Using some of the stuff on the Web can be a daunting experience! Some of it is **horrible**! Example (*though I am sure you could insert your own*): Last week, I tried to use the Web to look for a hotel in San Francisco. Lots of sites **claim** they will find you a room and make the reservation. Since I had time, I explored a few of them. One was worse than the other! On some sites you were forced to reenter data (*dates*) for every hotel you wanted to investigate. Didn't the programmer know how to **save** the dates? Each site was different, but none was great. One listed only ten hotels. Another listed over 100. Some had no sort at all—it jumped from flea bag to Fairmont to flea bag. One site **claimed** to sort any way you wanted, but its sort routine didn't seem to work very well! While looking for that hotel in San Francisco, I found one that looked interesting until I saw it was located in San Diego! **What?**

Finally, after much frustration, I found an acceptable hotel. I entered all the necessary data including my Credit Card number and hit the "send" button. What happened? I got an error message! It didn't tell me at what point the error occurred. Had the reservation gone through? Where did my Credit Card number go? There was no telephone number so I could ask a person those questions. After much hunting I did find an E-mail address. I wrote immediately. So far, no answer! Didn't anybody connected with the site try to use it before it was foisted on to the public? Doesn't anybody there read their E-mail? Am I a happy user? Will I go back to this site again—ever? Guess!

The next day, I tried again. This time, I found a site that while a little inconvenient to use did list a large number of hotels and did provide some information about each. I entered all the necessary data and it worked! I got back a confirmation. I had a hotel room. Isn't the Internet wonderful?

So far, we have talked about making a product salable. Sometimes, the problem is not recognizing when a product **is** salable! Two examples:

- In 1974 I visited the UNIVAC laboratory in Blue Bell, Pennsylvania. Some of the engineers there were working on a new, radical product. It was a computer embedded in a machine that could read bar codes. The idea was to use these readers in grocery stores. The clerk would pass the item over the reader and the machine would **automatically** identify the item, display the price of the item, and tally the bill! Radical??? Actually, UNIVAC knew their major competitor, IBM, was working on a similar machine. UNIVAC had dumped millions of dollars into this project. It was **almost** ready for prime time; just a few more bugs to chase down. Then, and **only** then, the UNIVAC Marketing people entered the picture. They foresaw all kinds of problems: How do you put a bar code on a bunch of bananas? How do you force a small company in Portugal to put a bar code on every can of sardines? Will clerks have to spend each night putting new bar code labels on thousands of items? If only the largest grocery stores can afford one of these, how many can we hope to sell? Result: the project was killed. The millions of dollars in R&D went down the tubes. (*If you recall, IBM did quite well with their machines*.)

- A few years later, I visited the Sperry laboratory in Salt Lake City, Utah. The engineers there had a radical new product: A computer that was small enough to fit on a desktop! At the time, there were a few little known companies that were offering build-your-own computers that came in a kit. Some of my friends were into that hobby. They would spend long nights soldering wires and plugging in transistors. Some of them never got the computer (*toy*) to the point where the thing actually worked, others did (*finally*) get it going. They were then the proud (*and I do mean **proud**!*) owners of a contraption that could do practically nothing! "But it **worked**!" This machine in Utah, however, was a **real** computer! Okay, it wasn't as powerful as its larger cousins, but it was functional and it could do **real** work. And, **it fit on a desk!** Radical! Then, the Sperry Marketing people entered the picture. They did a study. They determined that the market for computers for hobbyists was already saturated. "Nobody but a hobbyist would want a computer in the home! What would they do with it?" They claimed there was no market for **small** computers. "If a company was willing to invest in **any** computer, they would want one that had more function than could **ever** be built into a computer that fit on a desk!" Besides, there was more profit (*and sales commission*) to selling a large computer than selling a small one. That project, too, was killed.

*(The next year, IBM introduced its "Personnel Computer" and history was made!)*

One more item on that thought of building a better mousetrap. My introduction to I/T came as a programmer working on the U.S. Air Force Strategic Air Command, Command and Control System. We were privileged to be using the biggest and most powerful computer ever built - and the very first one to be using transmitters instead of vacuum tubes. *(It was built by IBM.)* We were able to replace the pencils and paper and adding machines the Airmen had been using to defend our country. We provided a computerized system that was eons faster and more efficient. Wasn't that even better than building a better mousetrap?

I will close this chapter with an old joke *(though I am not sure if it is funny or sad)*. Some years ago, a man was sitting at home trying to dream up a "sure-fire-get-rich-quick scheme." He decided that there must be a market for a new *(radical)* soft drink. "How about," he said to himself, "a lemon flavored soda?" And so he tried. He concocted a formula and tried it on his friends. He called it "1Up." Some friends thought it was too sweet, others, not sweet enough. He tried again: "2Up." No success. He tried over and over: 3Up, 4UP, 5Up. No success. He gave it one final try: "6Up."

Failure again! Discouraged and broke, he gave in to what he thought was the inevitable: "What is not to be, is not to be!" He never tried again!

# SELLABILITY

Congratulations!  You have created a brand new product and you have determined that the product is salable. Now, you have to sell it! **People** sell. Yes, ads cause sales and Web sites cause sales, but they have to be created by **people**. Most sales are done one-on-one and face-to-face. Can anybody sell? No. There are some people who couldn't sell a dollar bill for seventy-five cents! Others can sell anything! A **good** salesperson can switch from selling computers to cars to laundry detergent and be successful in each case. What makes the difference? In my opinion, it's the person's temperament.  It involves patience, ability to create rapport, ability to communicate, and the ability to create confidence in both the seller and the product.

Let us examine the art of selling  because even in a feeding frenzy the person who knows how to sell will sell more than the person who knows not.

Some, but not all, aspects of selling **can** be taught:
1. presentation skills
2. details of the product
3. proven techniques

Presentation skills encompass more than just how to speak. The skill must also include preparation of the presentation material and preparation of the sales**person**. Appearance **does** count!

Some presentation skills can be learned and/or honed.  Example: Humor. Learn when and when **not** to use it and learn that all humor is  not appropriate. Learn how to tailor your presentation to your audience.

Once upon a time, all IBM salesmen wore dark suits, white shirts, and conservative ties. It wasn't a uniform (*but almost*). Then, someone realized that in some cases, the salesman didn't look like the customers, so new rules were applied. Now, at least at conferences, Polo shirts seem standard for IBM employees. It still looks funny, to me, to see IBM Vice Presidents giving a Keynote address with an open collar and no tie. What would Tom Watson say?  At one conference, a fellow attendee commented to me that now that IBM has gone casual, the only people at the conference wearing dark suits and ties were the Japanese!

Actually, even during the blue-suit era in IBM, that was only for their people who came in contact with the customers and were supposed to project the IBM Image. Whenever I went to the T. J. Watson Labs, where the Systems Programmers did the really creative stuff, I saw sandals and torn T-shirts.

The salesmen should know the details of the product they are trying to sell. If the prospective customer asks a question that can't be answered it raises all kinds of doubts in their mind. However, there is something **worse** than not knowing an answer: giving the **wrong** answer! If you don't know the answer, admit it, promise to get the answer quickly, and then keep your promise. If you don't know where to get the answer, you are in trouble! Moral: do your homework!

If the product is too complex for the salesperson to know **all** the details, your company may consider doing what IBM used to do. If the size of the perspective order warranted it, IBM would send out a sales **team**. Besides the lead salesman there would be a technical expert and an expert on the competition. Among them, they were ready to field any question that could come up.

There are books available on selling techniques (*assumption close, etc.*). If those books would be useful, use them.

It is not only physical objects that can be sold. Sometimes it is necessary to sell an idea, a concept, or a cause. The same principles apply.

When I was teaching the art of selling, I used to argue with my boss. He insisted that the proper, nay **only,** way to sell was to constantly remind the customer how **good** the product is and **why** the product is good. In my view, sometimes the best way to sell is to not even mention "good." Instead, tell them what the product **is** and **how** it can be used and **what** the results will be. "Infomercials" need not come only on a video. Using this method, you allow the **customer** to draw the conclusion that the product is **good**. That can be more powerful because the customer has utter and complete confidence in his or her own conclusions. What the salesperson says he will take with a few grains of salt. The conclusions he draws for himself are cast in concrete. Perhaps my views on this subject hearken back to when I was studying Anthropology. I remember a lecture in which we were told that the best way to introduce a new tool—like a broom—into a primitive culture was not to give a sales pitch on brooms, but simply to **use** the broom. In this way, you let the people draw their own conclusion that a broom was a useful tool. Soon, they would want to use one, too.

One item that is important to me is usually not covered in the texts on selling: **when** to push, how **hard** to push, and when **not** to push. (*Perhaps this is related to my last point.*) Consider this: Every person who sells is also a customer — somewhere. We buy clothing, cars, houses, etc. If **that** salesperson is too pushy, doesn't it turn you off? Remember the golden rule here, too. Do unto others! If you don't like what some other salesperson does, don't do it yourself! Don't turn off a customer by being over zealous! I believe as many sales are lost by selling too hard as are lost by not selling hard enough. Of course, you have to read the customer to know when enough is enough. That read can be tough! It's much easier to watch someone else and tell when **they** have crossed the line.

As examples of excellent speakers (*salesmen*) who sometimes cross that line I offer these three:

- **BILL GATES**

  I have attended more of his presentations than anyone else's, probably because he gave more presentations than anybody else. His name always drew a crowd. His presentation was usually low key, his natural charm and enthusiasm comes through, he makes good use of humor—even if it's self-deprecating—and he doesn't hog the stage, he allows others to share the spotlight. That usually works well for him. Once I saw him change his style. That didn't work at all!

  **FALL COMDEX**, 1990 (Las Vegas) The conference opening Keynote Address was held in the Grand Ballroom of the Las Vegas Hilton.  In introducing Gates, the Master of Ceremonies said, "Bill packs this Ballroom just the way Elvis used to."

Gates reviewed the dramatic advances in the whole industry. This was the speech that introduced his concept of "information at your fingertips." "You need seamless integration." An amusing video dealt with living with a computer in the future. (*In the video, no commitments were made and no technical details were revealed—but it did provide the talk with sizzle. The audience enjoyed it.*)

**SPRING COMDEX**, 1991 (Atlanta)

Bill's session was held at 4:30PM, after everybody had already had a full day and their energy levels were running low. (*That can make it tough on a speaker.*) Gates received an ovation before he said word one. (*Windows 3.0 had just sold four million copies after being on the market for just one year.*) Gates was smiling. (*We all understood why.*) He discussed the reasons for Window's success. He didn't try to sell it because he didn't have to! He did say, "We need thousands and thousands of applications." He also promised that, "Windows 3.1 will be released by year-end and will respond to customer feedback." Smart move! (*Smart to do it and smart to tell this crowd they were **going** to do it*.) The audience applauded loudly. In spite of the scheduling, this was a successful Keynote.

**FALL COMDEX**, 1991 (Las Vegas)
The line for the Gates presentation started forming hours before it was scheduled to begin. Not everyone could fit into the Hall. Some who had waited over an hour were then turned away.

The stage setting was a computer store. (*Gates was not about to repeat the presentation he had given in Atlanta a few months before*.) "Today's computers are not only cheaper, they are dramatically better." The audience agreed. "There are more than 6.5 million copies of Windows sold." (*Now that's impressive*!) He offered a few demonstrations that kept the audience entertained while his soft sell took effect. He didn't need a hard-sell, he let the demonstrations speak for themselves. "We have made excellent progress over the last year." (*Obviously*!)

**FALL COMDEX**, 1992 (Las Vegas)

"Even the slowest applications look great on a 486!" "We don't need all that performance just to do the things we do today." "Over one million copies of Windows are sold every month." (*So, sales rose exponentially!*) Gates brought out people from other companies to demonstrate their own products. Then, a young boy was brought out to demonstrate "Encarta." (*The demo of the encyclopedia was much more impressive than any hard-sell could have been. Very clever and **very** effective!*)

**DB/EXPO**, 1993 (San Francisco)

"For the next decade—at least—PCs will double their performance every two years at no increase in price." Gates talked about the future as he saw it. Though that included Microsoft products, it was not limited to them. "We will see dramatic changes in database performance and in communications." He said there will be a whole host of vendors for both hardware and software. "That allows innovation to move at high speed." Eventually, he concluded, "we will have a full realization of the information age!" (*There were no hard-sell product commercials. It was another successful performance*.)

**FALL COMDEX**, 1994 (Las Vegas)
"Many people predicted that the PC market would reach saturation." (NOTE: *They have been saying that for quite a few years now*.) "The key to growth is innovation." "We have lots of frontiers to conquer." He used an entertaining video during which he spoke to the characters in the video. At the beginning of this presentation, Gates promised that it would not be about Microsoft. He kept his promise. What he did do was to announce at the end of the presentation that there would be a press conference, at a different location, immediately after this talk and that all were welcome. Clever move! If you wanted the Microsoft hard sell, and some people did, you were welcome to attend.

**NETWORLD+INTEROP**, 1996 (Las Vegas)
The conference opened with a keynoter that was bound to draw a

crowd: Bill Gates. Unfortunately, Gates left his tried-and-true formula of entertaining while providing a soft sell. This time, he tried a hard-sell. It didn't work. There was grumbling in the audience. While Gates was still talking, there was a line of people waiting to get **out** of the auditorium! This was the only time I saw Gates fail to win the audience. Here, he lost them—**big** time!

**FALL COMDEX**, 1996 (Las Vegas)
Gates went back to his formula for success. He talked about Intel, the Internet, and the Web. He downplayed Microsoft and Microsoft products. He showed a very entertaining video of people's reactions to PCs. In one vignette, the narrator—obviously a salesman— used obtuse technical jargon to talk to people. He received back only blank stares until he talked to a 10-year-old boy. The kid not only understood him, but could ask questions in the same language! The audience roared! Good keynote!

**CA WORLD**, 1998 (New Orleans)

The crowd for this presentation was so large it overflowed into an adjacent room. "Companies have to think about how to change the way they work." Referring to the Microsoft newly announced goal for simplicity, Gates made fun of some of the Microsoft error massages. The audience heartily agreed with him! "We have to make our own products simple." A very funny video drove his point home.

**FALL COMDEX**, 1998 (Las Vegas)

This Sunday evening presentation played to a (*naturally*) packed house. Gates opened with another very funny video. This one showed his trials and tribulations of the past year: pie-in-the-face, a demo that crashed, legal battles, digs from Scott McNealy. "The bug in that demo was fixed that night!" The audience appreciated that he would show us the famous bug-in-the-demo debacle and we were impressed to learn that it was fixed so quickly.

"We foresee incredible performance and fantastic advances." Gates showed off some Windows CE applications in cars, televisions, PDAs, etc. A few more short entertaining videos kept the audience amused. No wonder people like his presentations! They are fun! And, he doesn't mind getting a few laughs at his own expense.

- **STEVE JOBS**

Super-salesman! Virtuoso on a mouse! Terrific speaker! Showman! Only problem: he never **stops** selling! Examples

**DB/EXPO**, 1992 (San Francisco)

The title of his keynote was listed as, "Object-Oriented Programming in the 1990s." What he actually delivered was a straight sales-pitch for NeXT computers. He didn't just deliver it, he threw it at us! Hard! His energy and enthusiasm were almost contagious. He had the house lights turned off. He was not only the center, but also the **only** attraction visible! His performance on stage could have been used in a sales training class as a sample of a **perfect** hard sell. The audience was fascinated! We watched him create material using only a mouse. Then he made alterations on the fly. He did a week's work in three minutes! Fantastic performance! Great theater! But, it wasn't a keynote. Certainly it wasn't the keynote promised in the brochure. What it was was a remarkable demonstration of mousemanship!

**FALL COMDEX**, 1992 (Las Vegas)
The title this time was "CEO Perspective." Jobs' claim: "NeXT software is the only serious challenge to Microsoft." The mousemaster proceeded to give basically the **same** presentation he had given in San Francisco. He does it so well, he is so impressive, that the audience periodically interrupts him with applause. His software looks **magnificent**, but I wondered if someone other than Jobs could make it sing along at the same pace.

**DB/EXPO**, 1993 (San Francisco)
The lines for the Jobs keynote were as long as those for Gates'. Jobs gave the same presentation **again**! Same

slides, same jokes, same masterful performance.

- **CHARLES WANG**

  Excellent speaker. He can win over an audience with his charm and wit. He is particularly good at the CA World conferences where he is **expected** to praise his company and its products. Examples:

  **CA WORLD**, 1997 (New Orleans)
  "CA has been able to work a lot of magic in the past year." The theme of the conference became "magic." That theme was then skillfully carried through the five-day conference. Wang continued, "Magic is driving what seems technologically impossible."

  Wang described and praised a variety of CA products. Then, he described his involvement with "Operation Smile," a project to reconstruct children's faces that were deformed from birth. He gave a moving presentation.

**CA WORLD**, 1998 (New Orleans)

A full orchestra and a large troupe of dancers opened the keynote session. Small groups of them performed traditional music from various countries. The music began to overlap until it was impossible to distinguish any single piece. Result: discordant cacophony! Enter Charles Wang. His point: We have to work **together** in harmony or the result is chaos! "Let the world sing **one** song." (*Now that, folks, is how to make a point*!)

"This is the largest jam-session ever!"

In business, he said, "saving money is great. We have to decrease costs and squeeze out inefficiencies. But companies aren't just about saving money." He listed business goals: increasing customers, increasing revenue, raising quality, etc.

"We must make sure that upper management understands that I/T is an **investment**, not an expense."

"The world is complicated, messy, chaotic." Solving problems, he said, will require out-of-the-box thinking.

That was used as a lead-in to discussing a new CA product. (*Well done keynote*!)

**CA WORLD**, 1999 (New Orleans)
Wang made a spectacular entrance on a motorcycle. "The theme of this year's conference is The Fun of Software."

It was a fun presentation. The audience appreciated it.

Not every Wang presentation is so successful. Despite being such a good speaker, Wang has a tendency to sometimes push **too** hard. Example:

**INTERNET EXPO**, 1996 (Chicago)
"This (*the Internet*) is the hottest technology since the invention of the light bulb!"

"The Internet has made its name on its **potential**. It promises to revolutionize the way we do business."

He was doing great! He really had the attention of the audience. Then, he moved into a hard-sell commercial for CA products. He **completely** lost the audience! People started walking out while he continued to speak. He just didn't know when to quit! When you antagonize and audience—or an individual customer—you aren't going to sell them **anything**!

There are a few other well-known speakers who are excellent salesmen and are a study in contrasting styles. It's not the **style** that counts as much as what you **do** with it. Examples of three contrasting styles:

- **Scott McNealy** is an excellent speaker and excellent salesman. He makes good use of humor. When he slips in digs at Bill Gates and Microsoft, which he always does, they come out funny but **nasty**. His humor is acerbic, but the audience always gets a few good laughs.

- **Sanjay Kumar** also likes to slip in digs at Bill Gates and Microsoft, but his digs are delivered in good nature and with good humor. You get the feeling that Gates, who doesn't mind poking fun at himself, would enjoy the digs as much as Kumar does. (*He laughs along with the audience.*)

- **Larry Elison,** too, peppers his presentations with digs at Gates and Microsoft. In fact, sometimes it seems they are his main topic! Unfortunately, his digs are nasty without being funny! On one occasion, the audience booed his comments because they were a little **too** nasty.

There is one more product salesman I want to mention. His presentation was very good, but that is not the reason I am including him here. The reason to include him in this treatise on sellability is a single point that he made. This is something that just **had** to be passed on to you:

- **Draper Jaffray** from Digital River (*at the SPA-Europe Conference in Cannes, France, 1998*) told us that his company keeps their help desk open and available 24 hours a day, seven days a week. Do they get many calls at 3AM? No, very few. But, he pointed out, they **love** it when one does come through. Why? Because if you can answer a question or solve someone's problem at 3AM, you will have that person as a customer for **life**. They will **never** go elsewhere! Great point!

A few other speakers certainly deserve honorable mention. These men are purveyors of **ideas** rather than physical objects. Note the differences in styles—yet **all** are extremely good.

- **Bob Lucky**

  I have seen about a half dozen of his presentations. All were different – all were successful. The audience always appreciates his easy-going style and free use of humor. He always gets his points across. In the 1996 CIO FORUM, he said, "The Internet is an overnight success that started 25 years ago."

- **Gideon Gartner**

  His presentations are intense. He uses rapid-fire delivery to hammer home point after point. If you don't pay close attention, you are soon lost. If you **do** pay close attention you are rewarded by benefiting from one of the keenest minds in this or any industry. A Gideon Gartner presentation is an experience!

- **Ed Yourdon**

  As Gideon Gartner is intense, Yourdon is laid-back. He is excellent as both a speaker and as a host for a conference. His conferences are well run and he manages to put both the speakers and the audience at ease. His friendliness comes through. He makes the conference a pleasant place to be.

- **Dr. Vinton Cerf**

    His presentations are always well received. He speaks with dignity and authority. In discussing the Internet at the **INTEROP/EUROPE CONFERENCE** in Paris in 1993, he recalled that "even ARPANET couldn't afford the latest computer every year." His advice: "Don't get tied to any particular technology. Technologies change and disappear, but the Internet persists."

- **Jimmy Carter**

    The ex-President was never known as a "great communicator." However, when I saw his presentation at the 1999 **CA WORLD CONFERENCE** the rest of the audience and I were struck by his sincerity and humanity. He said that as President he was responsible for maintaining peace. "We never fired a bullet, dropped a bomb or fired a missile at anyone." (*The audience applauded.*) "Now that

I am involuntarily retired, I devote my life to a different kind of service."

"Most people in the world are poor." He described the work of the Carter Foundation and his involvement in the Habitat program. At the close of his presentation he received a standing ovation.

- **Tom DeMarco and Tim Lister**
  When it comes to presentations or seminars, they are the dynamic duo! Their most frequent topic is Project Management. Their views are original and, frequently, do not sit well with stogy, entrenched management. Tom & Tim ask people to do things differently—to change. That can be very unpopular advice. Tom & Tim manage to deliver their advice with grace and **lots** of good humor.

  During 1995 they toured the country with their seminar, "**Achieving Best of Class**." To give you the flavor of their routine, here are just a few of their points (*if you want to apply them to sales situations, feel free*!):
  "Avoiding risk is a sure way of avoiding opportunity."

"People have to be heroes to say something may go wrong."
"The 'can-do' attitude in the United States can actually harm a project. It's a cowboy attitude. It leads to the Titanic effect: you can't even **think** about icebergs!"
"Don't associate risk with 'bad.' Doing only safe things is a dopey idea!"
"All the projects with benefits and no risk were done **years** ago."
"The technical people see things that the manager doesn't."
"Everyone knows that using three people for six months is not the same as using six people for three months, but how unequal is it?"
"Most organizations don't do estimates. They set goals (*which are usually unrealistic*) and then try to meet them!"
By adding a person to a project you may **decrease** productivity.
"Debugging is like making love to an 800 pound gorilla. You

don't get to stop when **you** want."

In a project, "don't ask people where they **are**, ask them how much they have left to do."

"Ship happens! At some point, you have to ship!"

People assume that an effective short-run solution will also be effective in the long-run. T'ain't necessarily true! Example: a little alcohol may ease some pain, but more alcohol will not alleviate it. Other short-run solutions that may work (*only in the short-run*) include:  yelling at people, patching software, using pressure to motivate, working overtime.

Most people hate change. But, "you can never improve if you can't change at all."

At one of the Fall Comdex Conferences, we overheard two of the hotel people complaining that COMDEX attendees do not gamble much on the Casino floors. (*That's why the hotels charge so much during COMDEX.*)  Of course not! They spend all day on the Exhibition floor figuring our what to buy and what to ignore - that is a form of gambling, too! There, too, the problem is "when to hold 'em and when to fold 'em!"

# <u>COMPETITION</u>

Know thy enemy! At least know something about the market you are in and the companies and the products you are competing against.

In the past, I worked for two different companies that had vastly different views on competition:

- IBM

    I worked in a good-sized Department whose sole function was to monitor the overall Market, the major competing companies (*The market was known as "IBM and the seven dwarves."*), and the individual products competing against ours. There were analysts who specialized in each area. My area was the total Marketplace. I reported to Gideon Gartner. (*If you wanted someone to keep track of the Market, could you find anyone **better** than Gideon?*) We produced monthly reports, a mammoth yearly dissertation, and gave periodic briefings. It was important to IBM Marketing and to Product Planning to know what was happening and who was doing what to whom. Makes sense!

As mentioned before, sometimes one of the analysts from this department would be sent as part of a sales team to get an order. The analyst was prepared to give a blow-by-blow and detail-by-detail comparison of the IBM equipment being bid against whatever the competition was offering. Usually, the competition got blown away!

Some of the Analysts would attend the various conferences. (*Back then, they were called "Trade Shows." Remember? When did that become a dirty word*?) By simply walking the show floor they were able to garner information about the competition. (*They would garner for Gartner. Sorry Gideon, I couldn't resist that*!) No cloak-and-dagger stuff was needed or ever sanctioned. IBM would never deal in illegal data. That would have been against the character of the company. What's more, it wasn't necessary! You go to a conference, you ask a question, and you get an answer. Easy!

One of IBM's great advantages back in those days was really very simple: they knew more about the market and their competition than any of their competitors did. IBM could **act**. Some of the competitors could only react. Some never even got around to doing that! Unfair? Not at all! A better way to describe it would be, "Smart! Good business!"

- UNIVAC

*(When I joined the company, that was its name. Later, it became, SPERRY UNIVAC. Then, some Marketing guru decided that "UNIVAC" sounded too old and stogy, so it was dropped and the company became plain SPERRY. When that company joined with Burroughs (another of the original Seven Dwarfs) it became UNISYS.)*

The first thing I did upon arriving at UNIVAC was to inquire about their Department for keeping track of the Market and their competition. Do my dismay, they didn't have one! What was worse, in my estimation, was that they didn't **want** one! I learned that they had excellent engineers designing their equipment—some were with the company since the days of ENIAC! They were dedicated engineers. Dedicated to producing the equipment they thought the customers **should** have. Their attitude seemed to be that if the customer wasn't satisfied with the equipment they designed, it was because the customer didn't know any better! It never occurred to them that if they knew what the customers **didn't** want or use, they might be able to eliminate those features and thereby reduce the cost, lower the price, and become more competitive! That was never part of their game plan! Nor did it occur to them to find out what the customer really wanted or needed and then **add** those features—thereby making the product **more** competitive. Their attitude was a variation on Father-Knows-Best. Sometimes, Father hasn't got as clue!

You might say that working in this manner was either:
a) "working in isolation," or
b) "working with your head-in-the-sand," or
c) just plain "stupid!"

Take it for granted. Nowadays, whether or not you are watching your competition, they are watching **you**! How are they getting information about your company, your Marketing practices, and your products? Basically, five ways:
1. at Trade Shows (*Excuse me, Conferences*)
2. from your own Marketing material
3. from articles about you and reviews of your products that appear in the Trade Press
4. from your sites on the WWW

5. from your customers—especially the unhappy ones

If you don't know **who** your competition is or what you are competing against, you **can't compete!**

# SECURITY

**Question**: What has Security got to do with sales?

**Answer**: A lot !

Oh, sure! If you have never had a security problem, you may not see the connection. But, you don't know whether or not you will have a security problem **tomorrow**, so take a few minutes to consider a few facts.

A breach of your security could result in:
1. a major disruption of your business
2. a major disruption of client relationships
3. a loss of market share
4. negative publicity

See the connection to sales?

Think about these facts:

• From THE COMPUTER SECURITY INSTITUTE CONFERENCE, 1993 (Anaheim)

> Twenty years ago, computer security was much different. "Computer Rooms" could be locked and access could be limited to

those professionals who had a definite need for access. Thirty years ago, **all** the computer users were professionals. Control was much easier! Today, **everybody** uses a computer. The risk of a security breach has grown exponentially!

Often, top management doesn't appreciate the risks and they are reluctant to allocate funds to deal with security when they don't see the need. (*Security is an expense until you are glad you had it. Then, you look back on it as a wise investment.*)

There is often a lack of understanding about the need for security that can pervade the entire organization. To many on the staff, security just gets in their way.

Management is concerned about productivity. If security interferes with productivity…

The security risk from your own employees is about equal to the risk from outsiders.

- From the seminar, "PROTECTING YOUR BUSINESS LIFELINE," 1993 (San Francisco)

The instructor, John G. O'Leary, pointed out that people always wanting the latest and greatest hardware and software exacerbate the problem of security. And they also want quick access to everything, too.

Additionally, everybody wants to be trusted to do the right things. "People resent controls."

But, "people still make mistakes." More and more people are being given access to our networks. Each new person represents a new possible danger.

The more dependent you are on your networks and systems, **the more vulnerable you are.**

Sometimes it's difficult to convince people that the risks are real and get them to cooperate in security.

"Don't wait for things to happen. Plan ahead!"

Among the things to be ready for are:
   a) accidental disclosure of data
   b) accidental modification or destruction of data
   c) an unavailable or non-functioning network
   d) theft of equipment or data
   e) natural disasters

f)  sabotage
g)  equipment failure
h)  errors and/or omissions
i)  overwhelming complexity
j)  variations in coverage (*what is secure in one situation may be insecure in another*)

"One hundred percent security is impossible. There will **always** be some element of risk."

O'Leary reviewed the standard, but often ignored, security precautions: encryption, identification and authorization, etc.

To make security work, you have to win "the hearts and minds" of the people using the sensitive stuff. "They will comply **if** they believe it's in their own best interest to do so."

When evaluating the level of your security, don't forget to include any special situations brought about by Outsourcing.

Later, I attended another seminar that just dealt with Firewalls. If you want details on anything to do with security, there are books and there are consultants. My point is: don't overlook it and think somebody **else** should worry about it. Do you want somebody tampering with your Customer

List or any of the files you need to do your job? No! Do you want a breach of the company's security to turn into a catastrophe for **you**? No! Then satisfy yourself that somebody **else** really is looking after this stuff for you and make sure you are comfortable with the protection you have and the plans that exist for dealing with the situation when and if something goes wrong. Don't be shy. Don't be sorry. Look into it! Protect yourself!

# SUPPORT SERVICES

Our industry is unique! If you buy a new Toaster and it doesn't toast to your satisfaction, do you call toaster support? If you buy a new Iron and you don't know how to make the steam come out, do you call Iron support? No! But if you buy new hardware or software and you don't know how to connect it or it doesn't do as much as you expected, you call System Support! The vendor has to support System Support—and it's **expensive**! Not all vendors provide the same quality of support. Some give free support, some charge. Some have 800 numbers, some don't. Some answer your call immediately, some let you holding the phone for a week. Some recognize that the support they provide can enhance customer satisfaction and even provide valuable data to Sales and Marketing, some don't.

A seminar presented by the Help Desk Institute in 1996 in San Francisco offered some interesting insights. To wit:

> "Don't get caught up in the belief that automation can replace people." (*I hate those automated phone systems where you just can't get to a person! You can't ask an automated system a question! Additionally, I*

*hate going through five or ten voice menus
to get to the **right** person when I could have
told an operator in two seconds where I
wanted to be connected. Automated systems
may save money, but at what expense to
customer satisfaction?)*

There are some good systems being used by
Help Desk people that can assist in
providing customer service. "A Call
Management System is used to track calls
and problems. It is the core component of
most Help Desks or Support Centers."
These systems can provide a variety of
useful functions:
a) track calls and problems
b) track customers
c) verify customer status
d) track bugs and fixes
e) do inventory management for parts
f) do administrative functions—
notifications, reports, etc.

There is a large selection of these support
packages available. But, we were warned,
many of them are bought and never used.

These systems can be used in a proactive
manner: they can determine which
customers are likely to have the **same**
problem and provide advance warning.

*(Wouldn't that impress your customer! You fix the problem **before** they experience it! Maybe it's a little like a recall for cars.)*

A separate system is the Knowledge Management System. It helps your Help Desk people help your customers. "These systems provide tools for fast, accurate and consistent prevention and resolution of problems." They:

a) capture knowledge
b) organize the data
c) provide access to the data
d) present the data

"Support technology can reduce cost, increase revenue, and improve customer satisfaction all at the same time!"

When you do call a Help Desk you are never quite sure what support you will get. Some of the people that man those desks are terrific! They can walk you through your problem and lead you to the promised land! *(It must be a tough job! Not only do you have to be an expert on a lot of things and a good communicator, but you also have to put up with the public—that might be the toughest part! Example: an irate woman called to complain that her brand new computer had not been configured properly. They had failed to include a slot into which she could insert her CDs. "The only thing they added was the little pop-out cup holder!")*

The Help Desk people can alert Marketing to the needs of the customers (*in general*) and alert Sales to the needs of a **particular** customer. Best of all, they can, all by themselves, provide customer satisfaction. That's always good for business!

Moral: Marketing and Sales should support their local Support Groups because the Support Groups can support **them**.

# USER GROUPS

What's with User Groups? When you buy a pair of shoes, do you join a User Group?

Years ago, I used to attend the User Group meetings put on by IBM (*they had three separate Groups: COMMON, GUIDE, AND SHARE depending on the size of the computer they were servicing.*), UNIVAC, and Digital Equipment Corporation. Each company used its User Group differently:

- IBM

    IBM did the best job. They got **value** from those meetings. They allowed their customers to get together, compare notes, and gripe about what they didn't like. Then, IBM would evaluate the gripes (*they would evaluate worthiness of the complaint, extent of the problem, time to fix, cost to fix, etc.*) and report their findings back to the customers. Even if IBM elected to **not** fix something, they showed that they were willing to **consider** the fix. That provides a lot more satisfaction to the customer than if the complaint was just ignored!

Additionally, these meetings allowed the customers to get together and compare notes on what they **liked** about products and give each other advice on how to better use them.

The final thing IBM gained was **information.** It was information about what their customers wanted, needed, and expected in future products and as improvements in existing products. IBM Marketing gained insight into the direction of the market. Valuable stuff!

- UNIVAC

    It seemed that to UNIVAC, their User Group meeting was a disrupting and expensive necessity that they would have much preferred to do without. Since IBM did it and the customers expected it, they held a User Group meeting each year. They would get a few of their Marketing people to talk about a few of their upcoming products and they would offer an open bar. That was about the extent of it. They did not seem to be really interested in their customer's complaints or suggestions. They would patiently **listen** to complaints, but if you watched closely you could almost see the information going out the other ear!

The result was just as UNIVAC knew it was going to be, it as a self-fulfilling prophesy: it was disruptive because so many of their people had to be away for an entire week and it was definitely expensive. What did UNIVAC **gain** from these meetings? Nada!

- Digital Equipment Corporation

  DEC's attitude toward its User Group (*DECUS*) was entirely different from the other two. For them, the Meeting was an opportunity to have many of their customers together in the same place at the same time. So, what did they do? They gave Sales Pitches. The meeting was a DEC bazaar. There were displays, demonstrations, and sales talks. DEC provided a pleasant atmosphere, free food, and kept their customers hopping from one booth to another. A bazaar can be fun! If the meeting resulted in enough sales then it was all worthwhile!

  A little ancient history: here are some of my notes from the DECUS meeting held in Anaheim in 1987 (*Gee, Dad, did they* **have** *computers way back then*?) :

  "It is a Mecca for souvenir seekers. In addition to the pens that say 'DEC' and the key chains that say 'DEC' and all the different buttons that say nice things about DEC, there are Marketing Glossies galore and there are books about DEC and DEC products. DECUS thoughtfully provides sturdy shopping bags for attendees. People walk around with a shopping bag in each hand and both are loaded to overflowing. This conference is good exercise!"

"It's a selling orgy! The DEC staff is not there just to impress; DEC wants to **sell**! There are DEC salespeople all over the place—if you stand in one spot too long, they are all over you!

There is a:
a) DECUS store where you can buy many things that say DEC or VAX or DECUS. To do your Christmas shopping, you could even buy a reindeer that is labeled DEC for only $15!
b) DEC bookstore for DEC manuals and other DEC publications
c) DEC software shop where you can buy DEC software for your DEC hardware

d) Cassette counter to purchase a cassette recording of any of the sessions at the conference

e) special counter to purchase super-duper hardware specials available only to DECUS attendees

I sense a Batman syndrome here. The names of all the products are DECthis or VAXthat. They are probably manufactured in the DECcave and delivered in a VAXmobile!"

The following year I went to my first **Software** users conference: USENIX (San Francisco). Some of my notes:

"USENIX is an association of UNIX users—independent of any vendor.

I noticed a large billboard holding 'Employment Opportunities.' UNIX programmers are really in demand! Among the exhibitors at the show were two recruiting firms. Many of the vendors that were present had 'hospitality suites' to entice young programmers with their largesse. Beyond a technical conference, this appeared to be a recruiting conference—

close to Silicon Valley, where job-hopping is an art form.

The Keynote speaker, Dr. Adele Goldberg, CEO and President of ParcPlace Systems, told of her early experiences with UNIX—all **bad**.

The sessions were highly technical. This was a conference for working programmers so the level of detail was appropriate. The attendees managed to **look** like programmers. Dressed in shorts or jeans, some chose not to use the chairs, but to lay on the floor at the sessions. Obviously, they were **Systems** programmers. They listened carefully and asked incisive questions. They were learning and they were enjoying themselves.

In 1994, I want to Sun Microsystems "Software Developer's Conference" in San Francisco. My notes included:

The conference was to celebrate (*and to push*) Solaris (*Sun's Operating System*). There was a great line at the Keynote, "It's so easy you'd never know it was UNIX!"

McNealy provided some amusing digs at Microsoft. He went over big.

A variety of Sun speakers reviewed, detailed, and praised Solaris. A featured speaker, Steve Jobs, gave his usual impressive demonstration. He built a new application right there on stage and said, "See, you can do it in five minutes!" Not necessarily true! **Steve Jobs** can do it in five minutes. Mere mortals, who may not have built the same application over and over and practiced it with determined diligence, may take slightly or (*mightily*) longer.

There was not much at this conference for Management people, but for programmers learning or using Sun software, there was a lot! There were many training sessions and, what the programmers particularly liked, there was lots of **free** software. For them, good conference!

In 1997, I went to Computer Associates "CA WORLD" conference in New Orleans. It was so good, I went to it again in 1998 and 1999. From my notes:

- 1997

Our CA World experience began on the flight to New Orleans. Over half the passengers on that plane were going to the conference. Those who had never attended a CA World (*like us*) wanted to know, from those who had, what to expect. The word heard was 'fantastic!'

This was the year 'Unicenter TNG' was being introduced, so CA went all-out to impress the attendees. (*They succeeded.*) The CA speakers were all Support or Development people—not one speaker was from Sales or Marketing (*if you discount Charles Wang, himself*). That impressed us as a really **terrific** idea!

There was a wide selection of social events and plenty of free food and drink—even on the show floor. (*Of the three CA conferences we attended, this was the most lavish, probably because it coincided with the introduction of Unicenter TNG.*)

There were many training sessions and 'hands-on' sessions so you could try the software and get a 'feel' for what it could do. Additionally, each product group had a 'camp ground.' This was a fully equipped room staffed by development personnel. You could go there for a one-on-one session to ask questions or get advice or explanations. Or, you just might want to discuss the temperament and mores of the product. (*Great idea!*)

There were not **only** CA products on display or the subject of the sessions. The program was constructed to offer CA clients assistance wherever they might need it. Example: a session offering instruction on constructing a Web page taught the use of a Microsoft product.

Scott McNealy gave a well-received Keynote. On commenting why he was chosen to give the talk, he said, "I was cheaper than Bill Gates." McNealy suggested that since Microsoft makes a profit from support calls, they have inserted "randomly generated bugs so you call help at $36 a shot." (*Oh, come now, Scott. Be nice!*)

The next speaker was from Microsoft. He had only nice things to say about CA, Sun and Java. He said nothing about McNealy. (*He was nice!*)

The whole conference was impressive. There was hype, but that was to be expected at a vendor conference and it was appropriate to the occasion: CA was proud of its accomplishments. There was no hawking. There was a lot of training and education. There were, literally, **hundreds** of those sessions. It was a golden opportunity to get expensive training at an inexpensive price in a very pleasant atmosphere—and a little fun was thrown in just to make it even more enjoyable!

The organization and administration of the conference was outstanding. The staff did an excellent job.

Best feature of the conference? The attendees got to **experience** the technology. What a great way to learn and learn to appreciate.

- 1998

This year, there were five Keynote Addresses:
1. Charles Wang
2. Sanjay Kumar
3. Bill Gates
4. Eckard Pfeiffer
5. Rt. Hon. John Major

All the Keynotes were well received. Major ended his with a statement that I am sure Bill Gates appreciated, "Governments should get out of the way and let private businesses do their thing. Governments should not make market decisions."

This year, there were so many concurrent technical sessions that not even the large New Orleans Convention Center could accommodate them all. Many sessions were held in nearby hotels. There were also many pre-conference tutorials being offered. What made them unique from most conferences was that these were **free**!

The many one-on-one sessions with CA developers provided the users with an exceptional opportunity to learn and the users took advantage of that opportunity and appreciated it. Happy customers are **good** customers!

- 1999

On Sunday evening, before the official opening of the conference, there was a special meeting for the Industry Analysts in attendance. We each identified ourselves and told which company and/or publication we represented. I was surprised to learn that the Analysts from the United States were in the minority! Analysts were there from every continent. Later, I could observe that the Analysts were representative of the attendee population. The word "World" in the title for this conference was well chosen.

One session described a program that CA is experimenting with. It allows favored clients to work directly with the CA development team to insure that the client's needs would be met. That sounded like a great idea. The client gets to work with the Alpha version of the software. At that point, "the code may be shaky, but it is still relatively easy to insert changes." That must **really** please the client! And, "it gives CA the opportunity to see what **really** works in a real-world environment. We can get a better product to the marketplace and the customer is given early access to the product and can influence the features of the product."

CA described another program they were experimenting with—it, also, sounded like a great idea. If the client has an adequate number of employees trained and certified on a particular product, the cost of the maintenance contract for that product will be reduced. (*That makes a lot of sense!*)

Good conference! I am sure it benefited Computer Associates as much as it benefited the attendees.

Lesson to be learned: **If** you use a User Group conference wisely, you can gain great rewards. They are expensive to run. Make them an investment that will pay high dividends.

# SMALL ENTICING CONFERENCES

Oh ye purveyors of I/T-Ware overlook not these small gems of opportunity. The impresario is generally a respected Industry Analyst Group. These conferences usually attract between 100 and 400 attendees. That's all. They are relatively expensive and exclusive (*only the Brass gets to go to these*). These conferences are aimed at—and draw—upper management people. And, they are very focused. The attendees are there to concentrate on one particular aspect of their business and concentrate they do. (*The audience is always attentive and ready to ask incisive questions. They are also ready to debate the speaker if they disagree with something said. That tends to make these lively and interesting conferences. Sometimes, hearing both sides of an argument gets you a much better perspective on the subject.*)

There are three aspects to these conferences that should make them very attractive to you:

• The attendees

   If you examine the attendee list you will find that the vast majority of attendees are Directors, Vice Presidents, CEOs, COOs, etc. These are people with influence in their companies. If you win **their** hearts and minds you have won a major victory!

- The opportunity to show your wares

  To be sure, there will be no product commercials or sales pitches during the technical sessions at these conferences. All selling will be done off-line, in special areas reserved for personal contacts and in-depth questioning and deal-making. The conference schedules will not force attendees to sit through anything they would prefer to avoid (*like a blatant sales pitch*) or anything unrelated to the topic at hand. At these conferences there is no vulgar "exhibition." Here, they always use a euphemism. At Giga Information Group's "Business On Line Symposium" (*which was always an excellent conference with a good draw*) attendees are offered "Business ExChange Exhibits" (*small, tabletop displays*). Additionally, there is a "Cyber Village" where products can be examined in more detail and special arrangements can be made for additional demonstrations for the benefit of the home staff—at a convenient time and location. This is a great opportunity for vendors! If you can show products in keeping with the focus of the conference, you have delivered unto you an audience of top-level people—the decision makers. If you can, take advantage of these opportunities!

- The "Case Studies"

    A few Case Studies are always part of the program. A Case Study is a detailed look at some aspect of a company including **what** it does and **how** it does it—as well as how the company relates to the subject of the conference focus. It is **definitely** not a commercial for the company or its products. However, if the company and its prospects for success impress the audience there is definite advantage to be gained. So, if you can be a presenter and present a picture of your company and its efforts in a favorable light, you will be receiving the attention of that high-powered audience. (*Doesn't that sound enticing?*)

A few excerpts to serve as samples of quality:

- **The Commercial Parallel Processing Conference** (Gartner Group, 1995, Chicago)
    - Speaker: Donald Reinberg, Research Director, Gartner Group

"People are treating the database market as a commodity market. It isn't!"

When we get to 1,000 terabyte databases, "how do we manage those? How do we back them up?"

"The growing size of data warehouses, coupled with the need to coordinate data on handheld devices, is putting strains on manageability."

"Can you build a **huge** database? Yes. Will it run? Yes. Can you manage it? Not a chance!"

- Speaker: Arno Penzias (*Nobel Prize Winner*), Bell Labs

    "Computers are no longer irrelevant to business."

    "Systems are designed by experts to impress **other** experts."

    "Systems connected to other systems rarely work smoothly."

- Speaker: Richard Winter, Winter Corporation

    "The 'if you build it they will come' philosophy doesn't work! You need a **valid** business focus."

    "Unrealistic expectations or promises cause problems!"

"Identify all sources of risk. Get everybody's ideas of what they are worried about."
"Focus on the most critical risks."
"Don't waste time and energy looking for silver bullets."
"If a risk is major, don't wait. **Act!**"

- **Network & Distributed Systems Management** (Technology Transfer Institute, 1995, San Francisco)
  - Speaker: James Herman, Vice President, Northeast Consulting Resources, Inc.
    "The network management industry has been long on promises and slow on delivery. Users are frustrated. Many vendors have lost lots of money."
    "Unrealistic expectations have led to disappointment."
    "Some key standards have been missing and the competitive issues are too strong to get consensus at this point."
    "No one vendor sells enough to make back the major investment that is required."
    "Users are overwhelmed by the scale and complexity of their information systems."

"If a vendor can package knowledge, expertise, and experience, it will sell!"

- ■ Speaker: V. Desai, Goddard Space Flight Center
  "Every time you add a new piece to a system, there are more problems!"
  "Technology is great, but it's the people that make it work! They must be well-educated and well-trained. And, they must have the resources they need to make it all work."

- • **Business Process & Workflow Conference** (Giga Information Group, 1996, Lake Buena Vista, FL)

  - ■ Speaker: Raimund M. Wasner, President, Rheinner Group
    "Don't be fooled by what the vendor shows you."
    In discussing image processing, "It's not the speed of the scanner, it's the speed of the entire process that matters."

  - ■ Speaker: Bruce Cryer, Executive Director, Institute of HeartMath
    "Stress is one of the greatest inhibitors of business process effectiveness."

"In the current business environment, job security is an oxymoron."
"It is emotion, not intellect, which drives the business of the organization."
"Depression had doubled with every generation since the 1920s."
"One million people per day are absent from work due to stress-related disorders."

- Speaker: Gideon Gartner, Founder & Chairman, Giga Information Group
    "Knowledge has become a crucial corporate resource."
    "Knowledge is enhanced information."
    "The cost of knowledge has to be perceived as **less** than its value."
    "Information, by itself, it next to useless. We need a team of wizards, gurus, and diagnosticians— professionals with the essential experience—to produce a thing of value: knowledge."
    "Exclusive information has higher value than common information. It justifies a higher price."
    "People may be overpaying for information."

An intermediary is needed to sort through the flood of information available and convert it into a useful tool.

- Geoffrey Moore, author
  "The technology enthusiasts are the innovators that read Byte Magazine on weekends."
  He discussed the art of selling during the life cycle of a new product. In the early stage, do whatever it takes to get your foot in the door. Once the product enters the mass market, "turn yourself into a factory!"

- **Business OnLine Conferences**, Giga Information Group, San Francisco
  - Speaker: Larry Dietz, Vice President, Giga Information Group
    In discussing legal issues (*Dietz is an attorney*): "Don't confuse the legal system with justice."
    "The principle may be less important than the results."
    "Balance the legal issues with the practical business issues."
    "The law may not matter. The judge is the captain of the ship and social pressure is not invisible."

- Speaker: Bob Walker, CIO, Hewlett-Packard

    "We believe change is good."
    "A CIO has to be a cynical optimist."
    "Most people don't really want to manage their own PC [but] they don't trust anyone else to do it for them!"

- Speaker: James E. Clark, Vice President, NCR Corporation

    "Today's customers are demanding, critical buyers…and they are **not** brand-loyal."
    "All the technology stuff is getting better and working together."
    "We collect and analyze sales [data] by the market basket."
    "You want to know what **didn't** work, too!"
    "**Use** technology, don't abuse it!"

These conferences can offer a **unique** opportunity for you to influence influential people.

# SMALL REWARDING CONFERENCES

The sponsors of these conferences are highly respected organizations of I/T executives (*examples of such organizations: The Society for Information Management (SIM) and The Information Management Forum (IMF)*). These, too, are small conferences with a high-level attendee list and a narrow focus. No one would **dare** to try to sell at one of these conferences! However, it's a great opportunity to **impress**: you can show that you have competent management, a knowledge of your market, and know the direction that your company is aiming for. The goal for you would be impress **now**, reap the rewards **later**.

Here are samples from two conferences sponsored by the "Information Management Forum." These conferences are not open to the general public. They are presented for the benefit of the members of that organization. However, **prospective** members are allowed to monitor one conference. Each conference has a theme. (*These conferences are exceptionally well run. They are genteel: good hotel, good food, the pleasant company of colleagues.*)

These samples are from two of their conferences.

- Perceptions of the Future (Tucson)

  1. The speaker was Wendell Jones, CIO of the National Association of Security Dealers. "In the securities industry, mandated products and delivery dates leave little room for error. We work under the threat of contempt charges." (*And you thought you had it tough. Ha!*)
  2. The speaker was Dwight Gertz, CEO of Symmetrix.
     "There is an overemphasis on cost cutting which, by itself, offers diminishing returns and limited future value."
     "Firing people is a **lousy** way to attract the best people!"
     "Some companies engage in lay-offs year after year. They never seem to learn."
     "Fewer than half the downsizing companies increased operating profit."
     "Despite economic and competitive challenges, some companies are experiencing profitable growth."
     "Growth opportunities exist in every industry."
     "Which companies grow? The ones that do something **different**. Not better, **different**!"

- Moving Into The Future (San Diego)

1. The speaker was Todd Carlson, CIO of EDS. "The biggest single source of sustainable competitive advantage in the future will be our ability to create and mobilize knowledge in the interest of new products and services."
2. The speaker was Mike Hill, Vice President, IBM. "We have to take the confusion out of electronic business."

   Hill gave his definition of the role of the CIO:
   a) aligns the business process with I/T
   b) aligns I/T with corporate strategy
   c) develops global I/T strategies and goals
   d) establishes corporate data standards and architectures
   e) incorporates new technologies into I/T
   f) addresses change management

SIM treat their attendees with the same respect (*and kid gloves*) as does IMF. These conferences are truly a pleasure to attend—the sessions are interesting and useful and the social events are cordial. Here are samples from two Society for Information Management conferences:

- Piloting I/T Into Harmony With Business (Salt Lake City)

  The speaker was Jeanne W. Ross from the MIT Center for Information Systems

Research and the Worcester Polytechnic Institute. "There are four possible scenarios for I/T organizations:

1. extinction
2. being heavily outsourced
3. being largely distributed to business units
4. or, quite the opposite, having the whole business organization transfer itself into a giant I/T organization"

She claims that a good working relationship between I/T and business people "is essential!" The relationship should be strong enough to withstand I/T saying, "Well, it doesn't work yet, but it will soon." *(That drew a laugh, albeit a guilty laugh!)*

She suggested you carefully examine your own I/T organization. "You are unlikely to find that you are perfect."

Her closing remark, "Manage the pain that is **always** associated with change."

- CIO Forum (Rancho Mirage)

  The speaker was Nicholas Negroponte, founder and director of MIT's Media Laboratory and author. "You may have a market you don't know about and you may have competition that you don't know about."

It's only the large, usually international, companies that employ CIOs, but your competition can come from a tiny company in a remote location. "These tiny companies can do **terrific** business—and there are ten thousand of them out there!"

These speakers did not praise their companies, institutions or products. All they did was convey **useful** information and then leave the audience with a good impression of themselves and the institutions they represent. (*Advice: Go and do likewise.*)

# SMALL DELUDING CONFERENCES

Happily, there are few of these.  Shamefully,  there **are** a few of these. These are small conferences that delude the attendees into thinking they will receive benefit from attending and delude the vendors into thinking they will receive benefit from displaying. Neither is true. The only one to benefit from these is the conference sponsor.

The vendor is promised that the sponsor will deliver bodies. By purchasing booth space the vendor will also receive a time slot in the technical conference in which the vendor can present whatever they please. (*The presentation **always**, regardless of the title given to the session, becomes a sales pitch*.)  The innocent vendor (*Hey! Give them the benefit of the doubt. Call them "innocent"—at least at this point because, in this instance, they are the "dupee*.") signs the contract and shows up at the show. Usually, by the second day, the promised audience has left town, the bodies have flown the coop.

The ads and the brochures tell people what a marvelous and exciting conference this is going to be. When the conference begins, the attendees discover that the list of session titles they were given turns out to be complete fiction, for whatever the title, all they get is the sales pitch.

You have to recognize the trap **before** you make the trip or pay the registration fee. The clues should be:

1. If the price (*for vendor or attendee*) is so low that is sounds too good to be true, **beware!** (*The price may be low, but it certainly isn't "good!" In fact, the experience will undoubtedly turn out to be costly—for vendor and attendee alike!*)
2. If the speakers are **all** Managers, Directors, or Vice Presidents of Marketing, and there is no big-name keynoter or speaker on the program, **beware!**

I went to one of those nasty conferences just to investigate how bad it could be. My conclusion: **Very** bad! Every "technical" session was a sales pitch or some self-serving lecture that the speaker thought was for the aggrandizement of himself, his company, and/or his product. Boy, was he wrong! All he accomplished was to alienate the people in his audience. (*It certainly alienated me! The one bright spot for me was that, since I was writing a critique of the conference, they gave me a **lot** to criticize. Actually, writing them up as the **worst** conference I ever attended gave me pleasure! Ha! Take that!*)

On the first day, conference attendance was poor. On the second day, most of the audience had already left town. Even some of the scheduled speakers didn't bother to show up! Some of the vendors had caught on—a little late perhaps, but at least they recognized the error of their ways. Some of the booths were no longer manned. The tents had been folded.

As one unhappy fellow attendee said to me, "This conference is leaving a bad taste in my mouth!" The taste gets worse when you think about the time and the money you have wasted. Who can you blame? You will probably never hear of the sponsor again—they can assume a different name for each event. So, you blame the **vendors** that were there—even the innocent ones (*if there were any innocent ones—after all, they had accepted the time slot with malice of forethought*).

Planning, organizing, and bringing a conference to fruition takes time, work, and money. The sponsor is entitled to make a profit. Occasionally, some unscrupulous souls see this as an opportunity to run their scam, delude a lot of people, and make a profit that isn't strictly or legally dishonest, but certainly seems **morally** dishonest. It harms not only the attendees, who have wasted time and money, and the vendors, who have also wasted time and money, but it also hurts the **honest** conference sponsors. It hurts the reputation of conferences in general. And it casts a shadow of suspicion on **all** vendors.

Avoid these conferences like the plague! No smart vendor wants to be responsible for a dirty taste in anybody's mouth and no attendee wants to waste time and money either. (*Especially if there is nothing enjoyable about the whole the experience. Ugh!*)

If enough people perceive these to be the scams they are and refuse to attend or to participate in any way—like buying booth space—the scoundrels will **lose** money. Good! That's what they deserve! That should keep them from trying it again!

Moral: Caveat Emptor!

# MID-SIZED CONFERENCES

These mid-sized conferences are popular. More of them are offered each year then any other size. Many different companies (*impresarios*) present these conferences on a regular basis. (*Two of my favorites were Miller Freeman, Inc. and Digital Consulting, Inc.*) The conference agendas are semi-focused. They provide a broad treatment for a particular topic as long as it remains "hot," then the topic is dropped like a hot potato. Example: "Client/Server." That was an **extremely** popular subject—for a while. You never hear mention of it anymore.

Size does count, but it's not just the size of the audience that makes these conferences useful to you. Other considerations apply. They include:

*       The speakers
        At the **good** small conferences (*by "good" I mean the Small Enticing and Small Rewarding Conferences*) all the speakers are **invited**, that is, they are carefully selected by the sponsor. That means there is an element of control: poor speakers, dull speakers, or those who insist on giving product commercials are never

invited back. Many invitations are extended on the basis of prior reputations. Some speakers with exceptionally good reputations are invited frequently. At these mid-sized conferences, however, the **Keynoters** (*frequently more than one*) are invited, but some are still **volunteers**. That can present a problem for both the sponsor and the attendees. The volunteers can be disappointing—for a variety of reasons. People volunteer to give a presentation for many different reasons. For example:

a) They feel they have something important to say and want to expound on particular topic. (*As an attendee, or even as the sponsor, you may not agree that what they say is important. Or, perhaps it truly is important, but the speaker just doesn't know how to give a presentation.*)

b) They want to sell you something.

c) They want an excuse to give to their boss so they can make the trip to the conference. These people become painfully obvious. They show up, sometimes late, with few if any visual aids and no clear plan as to what they are going to talk about. Sometimes, they just throw it back to the audience, "What do you want to talk about?" In my view, they disgrace themselves. Unfortunately, they also disgrace the conference and, by association, the conference sponsor.

- The registration fee
    Here, the registration fee is less than at a good small conference, but more than at a deluding conference. The fee **does** influence the draw. Executives are willing to pay a high price for themselves, but are reluctant to authorize it for lower-level people—especially when budgets are tight (*as they usually are*).

- The attendees they draw
    Most attendees at these events are middle management or upper echelon technical types.

- The treatment of the attendees
    At the good small conferences, the attendees are pampered. The meals are included and are excellent. There is always at least one catered cocktail party. At the lower priced mid-sized

conferences, **if** a meal is included it's far from sumptuous. (*I remember one conference where it had been prominently advertised that lunches would be included. That was supposed to be one of the enticements. On the first day, the lunch was a soggy hot dog and a little bag of potato chips. On the second day there was some variety: it was the same soggy hot dog, but a **different** brand of potato chips. Whoopee!*)

At these conferences, the exhibition is sometimes actually called, "The Exhibition." Like the size of the audience, the exhibition is usually larger than found at the small conferences. Sometimes, there are elaborate booths to be found here. DCI had been holding two separate conferences at the same location and at the same time. Then, they co-mingle the two Exhibitions so that it appears to be one. (*It looks much larger that way. And, of course, it saves DCI some expense. Actually, it's a clever move. DCI had experience at cutting costs. They do a good job of it while still presenting rewarding conferences. They run a tight ship. The attendees, as well as DCI itself, are the beneficiaries.*)

These mid-sized conferences are aimed at a different audience. They aren't aimed at the executive level. Therefore, the approach of both the speakers and the vendors must be different. This audience will look for more detail about the technology—not just **what** it does, but **how** it does it.  We aren't at the bit-chasing level, but more detail is welcomed. In fact, the absence of any detail may be viewed with suspicion. These conferences can definitely be rewarding for both the attendees and the vendors if the speakers and the vendors have properly aimed their material at **this** audience.

Some of the presentations, particularly among the keynotes, can be excellent. There were a few speakers I always sought out:

- Dr. George Schussel, Chairman and CEO, DCI

    Schussel always forcefully takes a position on an issue. I frequently disagree with him, but I always appreciate the way he presents his case. He is never ambiguous! He lets you know **exactly** how he feels about an issue. (*For well over a year, we had an on-going disagreement. He presented his case at conferences and I presented my rebuttal in the CONFERENCE ANALYSIS NEWSLETTER. He insisted that using Client/Server technology would save* *money. I insisted that, though it may be extremely useful and worth the expense, it would **not** save any money. I was overjoyed to finally hear him say, at a DCI conference in Chicago, "The total cost per seat may be lower with a mainframe." Yea for our side!*)

- Max Hopper, Principal, Max Hopper Associates, Inc.

  He, too, is opinionated. "New technologies create not just an opportunity, but a survival imperative."

- Shaku Atre, Atre Associates

  Atre makes her points with biting humor. She is always outspoken and always entertaining. And, she offers some **excellent** advice. She frequently makes the point that when you are forced to work with different products from different vendors, "the dirt collects in the interfaces. It's my onion theory: the more layers there are, the more you are going to cry!"

- Colin White, President of DataBase Associates International

  He, too, is a forceful speaker who states his opinions unambiguously.

*(Unlike Schussel, I usually agree with White.)* "We are moving toward more openness (*in systems*) but I believe we will never get to a **true** open system."

- Ken Orr, Founder of the Ken Orr Institute

  Orr's presentation are fun! They are presented with charm, but never fail to make their point—strongly. "There is always a gap between what the gurus and the Press tell us about a new technology and the reality." "In a traditional database you can ask, 'What is…'" in a DataWarehouse you can ask, 'What if…'" At an earlier conference in New York City, he had commented, "We have more technology than we know what to do with. That leads to a **very** complex environment!"

- Larry DeBoever, Consultant

  He is always entertaining. Sometimes, he's a little crude, but he is never dull! He speaks his mind. "The best UNIX programmers are re-trained mainframe programmers." (*I believe that. UNIX is tough stuff*!) "End users lie! Vendors lie! And consultants lie, too!" When asked what he thought of a company's five year plan he responded, "You're out of your mind! You need a **two**-year plan!" (*What he lacks in charm, he makes up for in honesty!*)

All of the speakers listed above are outspoken (*which is probably why I like to listen to them*). That doesn't mean that **all** outspoken speakers are always right. As an example a forceful, outspoken speaker who was dead wrong on at least one occasion, consider Richard Finkelstein at the "Database & Client/Server World" conference in Chicago in 1996. He said, "PCs are obsolete!" He, and many others, thought that Network Computers would take over the world. Wrong! (*I argued that there was a small difference in price and a big difference in performance between and NC and a PC. The PC is definitely worth the small difference in price.*)

Sometimes, a speaker from outside our industry is invited to make a presentation. Usually, it is an author who has written about something **related** (*even remotely*) to the topic at hand. Always, it is someone who can grab and hold an audience. `Examples: Alvin Toffler, Carl Malamud, Geoffrey Moore, and Jimmy Carter.

There is something else all those speakers, **each** of whom can "capture" an audience, have in common: they don't try to **sell** you a product. They do try to sell you on an idea, but you don't have to lay out hard cash when you accept (*or reject*) their idea.

Then, do these conferences offer any kind of opportunity for a vendor? **Definitely**! They offer a **great** opportunity! The vendor should buy booth space at the Exhibition and schedule a session during the conference. The trick is to **not** sell during the session. Use the presentation to talk about the **technology**. You **know** that every paid attendee is interested in technology. Take advantage of that. Don't even **mention** a product. Focus, and get the audience to focus, on the **technology**! Then, at the close of your presentation, invite them to visit your booth for a demonstration of the technology in action. The **booth** is the place to do the selling! Will every member of the audience show up at your booth? Of course not! But that's Okay. Your **best** prospects will show up. They are the ones you want to concentrate on. Let the others wander off. Spend your time and effort where it is most likely to pay off.

When used correctly, these conferences can be a gold mine! They don't require a huge investment, but they can pay a large dividend.

# INTERNATIONAL CONFERENCES

**Every** conference is an international conference in the sense that there are always attendees from outside the United States. However, what I want to address here are conferences that are aimed at doing **business** outside the United States. Attending a conference can not only give you a general "feel" for doing business in a foreign land, it can also give you very specific tips and make you aware of potential problems, possible inroads, and even legal pitfalls and loopholes.

Examples:

- **COMDEX MIAMI**, Miami Beach, 1999

   As I wrote at the time, "Latin America is a sleeping giant of an I/T market." I have traveled throughout Latin America and I can testify that I/T is in some cases creeping and in other cases leaping into the daily life of the people. (*One example: While traipsing though a remote forest area of Costa Rica—with howler monkeys howling and colorful parrots swooping—we came across a charming little hostel accessible only by Jeep. Upon investigation, we were offered a brochure that gave us their Web-site address*.)

Where is a center of Latin American business? Where do all Latin American companies do banking and negotiate deals? **Miami**! This conference was held in Miami Beach. (*Latin Americans love to travel to Miami*!) This was **definitely** a Latin American conference.

Some sessions were held in Spanish, but most were held in English with simultaneous translation available for those who needed it. (*This was a concession because the conference was in Miami. In Latin America, local-language is extremely important. At this conference, most of the attendees needed that simultaneous translation*.)

The many useful sessions included these:

- The speaker: Oscar Jaramillo, President, InterMemory Corporation

    "Three options are available to you if you want to expand your business into Latin America: Start from scratch, buy an existing or established company, or enter into a joint venture with an already established Latin American company."

"You need to think about how you will get set up. For instance, billing can be a major problem. Will you use a local company or bill from your home office?"

How will you manage your business? Who will do it for you? "You need local talent."

"Make sure one person is in charge. Companies get stuck if there is nobody to make a decision."

"Every country has a **different** tax structure. You will need a good tax consultant." He warned that if you aren't careful, you could end up paying taxes twice: in the U.S. and in Latin America. "That can cause a serious cash flow problem!"

"There are currency and exchange rate issues to consider." They can acutely effect your profits and losses.

- The speaker: Andre Vanyi-Robin, President and CEO, Visualcom, Inc.
  "By next year, there will be more mobile phone-users in Latin America than in the U.S. That offers a great range of business opportunities."

"Dell has decided to go into Brazil to sell." He predicted they will face these obstacles: logistics, delivery, payment, and security. "Dell will find it difficult to fill their orders."

- The speaker: Moises Polishuk, President, Association for Systems, Security & Teleprocessing

> "We have helped Compaq, Microsoft, Hewlett-Packard, Novell, Unisys, Oracle, and others."
> "Resellers that add no value will die fast!"
> "Wholesalers are changing. They are establishing an infrastructure to enable them to deliver goods directly to the customer. They are getting closer and closer to the end-user."
> "Only the **best** will survive."
> "To succeed in Latin America you have to minimize employee turnover. It's a nightmare! Training is an ongoing situation."
> "The winners will have to pay attention to the opportunities."

- The speaker: Pat Martin, Corporate Vice President, Xerox Corporation

"Over half the growth in the Internet over the next five years will be **outside** the United States."
"Most Latin American companies are still behind in the use of technology."
"Technology alone is not the answer. You need **knowledge** to make things happen!"

- The speaker: Carlos Guzman-Parry, The Yankee Group

"The opportunities are growing rapidly!"
"Most long-distance opportunities in Latin America are being liberalized."

- **COMDEX/SUCESU** (Sao Paulo, Brazil, 1993)

This was the first COMDEX to be held in Brazil. The Interface Group (*at the time, they sponsored all the COMDEX conferences*) teamed with a Brazilian outfit, SUCESU, for this event. Unfortunately, SECESU had too much influence and the conference was not up to the usual COMDEX standards. I criticized the conference heavily in my CONFERENCE ANALYSIS NEWSLETTER and listed all the improvements I felt were needed. The Interface Group said the improvements would be made the next year and offered to send me back to Sao Paulo to verify that the changes were made. I was unable to accept their invitation.

At a private reception the night before the conference opened, the wife of a member of the United States Trade Commission told me, "Sao Paulo is the New York of South America. It is the center of commerce for the whole continent." (*Indeed it is an important center! But Miami is much more convenient!*)

Some excerpts:

- The speaker: Alvin Toffler, Author

> "Instead of a smooth transition to a global economy we have confusion and strife."
> "We are told to look for the most **probable** future, but some of the biggest changes come from **improbable** events! We need to examine the **possibilities**."
> "We are changing at accelerated rates."
> "If you have the right information, you can do a lot!"

"Knowledge is the ultimate substitute for many other factors. It has **enormous** implications. It effects **everything!**"

"In the Gulf War, an ounce of silicon was worth a ton of uranium."

"The most important possessions of a business are intangible. The real value is what's inside your head—not the machines, not the software."

"We are shifting from mass production to customization. ... It's a matter of pushing a few buttons to change a few lines of code. The price of diversity is going down."

"Money [*now*] moves at the speed of light [*electronically*]. Information has to move **faster!**"

■ The exhibition:

By COMDEX standards, it was small. Almost all demonstrations, sales literature, sales pitches, and everything else were in Portuguese. (*NOTE: In Europe, things computer-related are basically in English. In Latin America, everything is in the local language.*) For attendees who did not speak Portuguese, translators could be hired by the hour.

One American company had not been forewarned. All their material was in English and English-speakers manned the booth. They had to keep a translator at their side for the entire show. (*I wondered if their expense account listed that item as an "unexpected" or "unfortunate" expense.*)

The pizzazz of Las Vegas was absent. The "feel" of the show was entirely different. The "draw' was just as strong! The show hours were from 10AM to 10PM. Over 150,000 people passed through the gates!

The American exhibitors were all well pleased with the results (*except that one poor guy with the translator*). They felt the long trip was worth the expense.

The next year, The Interface Group presented **two** conferences in Brazil—which is certainly an indication that they felt the first one was a success. They went back to Sao Paulo and added a show in Rio DeJaneiro.

- The speaker: Roydon Olson, Novell

  "Brazil has one of the largest per capita mainframe installations in the world. The pressure isn't down-sizing, it's down-**costing**!"
  "Brazilian software products are becoming more exportable."

- **INTEROP/EUROPE** (The Interop Company, 1993, Paris, France)

  - The speaker: Ellen Hancock, Senior Vice President, IBM

    "Technology is the tool that makes dreams come true."
    We have to "manage the hidden cultural problems…face the cultural challenge. We cannot isolate ourselves or we will be out of business."
    "Governments can't be restrictive! They must allow free communication. The international borders are coming down."

  - The speaker: Dr. Galitsky, ELVIS (Russia)

It takes two years to get a telephone connection in Russia. "How do you start a new business and wait two years?" He claimed that the whole economy of the country is being held back by the lack of a communications infrastructure. (*Now they use cell phones.*)
"We will need E-mail, data-sharing, collaborative computing, and [other technical advances]."
"Russia is a good business opportunity. Over 55,000 small towns and villages have no communications at all!" *(Cell phones?)*

■ The speaker: Dr. Hubert Curien, French Minister of Research and Space

"People want to travel, to communicate, and to have links with society. Users want personalized information."
"Information becomes part of your work and part of yourself. Networks connect **people**. It is more than connecting locations."
He said that universities used to want to have large computers. That got to be very expensive. Now, they just

want to be **connected** to large computers.

In building networks, "you have to analyze and compromise."

"Some level of quality is enough. It doesn't have to be taken to extremes!"

"De facto standards are more important than legal standards." "If it **works**, it becomes a legal standard!"

- The speaker: Denis Yaro, Vice President, SunConnect

"It is impossible for American companies to succeed in Europe unless they have a presence in Europe. You have to be close to your customers [and] your business partners."

"If you stay in the United States, you have to wait for things to come to your attention."

"Expanding in Europe allows us to be more responsive to our customers in the United States."

"Technology will never remove the human element, you can't take that away. We can only use technology so much."

"There is need for face-to-face contacts."

- **NETWORLD+INTEROP** (Softbank Forums, 1997, Paris, France)

  - The Exhibition

    Large, colorful, and active. Well organized. More formal than in the U.S. The booth attendants (*and the attendees*) were better dressed.

    The bookstore stocked mainly books in English, but most of the demonstrations were in French.

    A touch of being in France: One of the prizes was a bottle of French wine. It was a "Chateau Latour"

  - The conference sessions and the included tutorials:

    Very disappointing! This was an American conference, and not a good one, that was held in France. There was nothing about doing business in Europe, there was no opportunity to learn about the state of the European market for I/T-Ware products. The trip was a waste of time and money!

- **The Software Publishers Association European Conference** (SPA, 1998, Cannes, France)

  - The speaker: Dieter Waudig, ASKnet, GmbH, Germany

    The European Union Value Added Tax (VAT) "does not apply **if** the [software] publisher is outside the EU." He said there is a rush, by some publishers, to establish themselves in Switzerland or the United States. "Then, they get to offer tax-free products."

  - The speaker: Dieter Giesbrecht, Symantec Ltd.

    "We are trying to be legal, decent, and honest. So, we keep buying **more** licenses!"
    "We waste money trying to count licenses!"
    "Having fewer providers saves money."
    "You expect us to control the licenses, but you don't make it easy. If you circumvent our Purchasing department, we lose control."

"Try reading a Microsoft licensing agreement. Ha!" (*The audience laughed.*)

"We need simple license rules that don't change."

"I want to reduce the total-cost-of-ownership."

"The vendors that work with me are the ones that I want to do business with."

"We don't want you to be the cheapest, we want you to provide the best **value**."

"Partnership is key!"

- During discussion periods:

  There were discussions about security and privacy issues. It was pointed out the laws can, and do, differ from country to country. Therefore, to avoid running afoul of the law, you need to know the law of each country in which you do business.
  Comments heard:
  "European law doesn't prevent you from collecting personal data, it just requires you to use it fairly."
  "The United States is **way** behind Europe in these matters!"

- **Software Publishers Association European Conference**, (SPA, 1995, Cannes, France)

This conference featured a special session on doing business in Eastern Europe. The session leader was Esther Dyson, EDventure Holding. Dyson is an Expert on the subject. It was an excellent, informative session. Among the comments heard were these:

> "Financial resources are very limited. Inventory levels are quite low. The cost of money is high."

> "The infrastructure for carrying on business is improving [rapidly]."

> International distributors are taking over from the local ones. Localization is expensive, but not always necessary.

> "You can't depend on distributors to advertise your product. You have to do that yourselves."

> "These countries are a big market for specialized products—like security.

> "Local communication lines are cheap."

"The big on-line service companies are not interested in Eastern Europe yet."
(*Apparently smaller, local companies are coming into their own. Dyson told us she owns one in Poland.*)

"We use common advertising across Eastern Europe. We just localize the text."

"You need to know what you are doing in Eastern Europe. You need a local distributor."

"Russia is a special market, but you can be very successful there."

"Russia is a jungle! To do business there, you need a bodyguard!"

(*Ester invited me to be a Keynote speaker at her next conference in Poland, but I had commitments here at home.*)

Don't attempt to do business in **any** foreign country until you have thoroughly researched the project. Learn the laws. Learn the obstacles. Learn the costs. Estimate the rewards. If, in balance, the project appears to be favorable, get help. Proceed cautiously. But, don't ignore the opportunities. Great fortunes can be made in small countries.

# REALLY BIG CONFERENCES

The very best place to observe the buying/selling feeding frenzy in action was at a Fall COMDEX. The activity was frantic! And Bill Gates, and others, took advantage of the great opportunity.

Which "Really Big Conference" comes to mind first? COMDEX! There are others, too, but COMDEX will easily serve as the model. These conferences are a feeding frenzy in action! Huge crowds. Loud noise. Color. Motion. Confusion. They have them all! What they no longer had after the first few years, I was told, was the high-level wheeling and dealing right on the show floor. The show floor was abandoned to the lower-level troops who don't have the authority to spend the big bucks. The big buyers spend all their time in the hotel suites where the demonstrations and the true negotiating were being done in private—away from the maddening crowd. That is where the booze and the high pressure selling was taking place and the "big bucks" were changing hands.

At these conferences, there are always crowd-pleasing keynotes. Most of the other technical sessions, however, run the normal bell curve of good-to-mediocre-to-bad. Why? Because we are dealing with volunteer presenters. Not all volunteers have pure motives or are good presenters.

The fun is on the show floor.

- **COMDEX**, FALL, 1990 (Las Vegas)

Way back in 1990, COMDEX was "the biggest Trade Show ever held in the United States!" It covered the space of **fifty** football fields, had 1,800 booths, representatives from 22 countries, and attracted "over 125,000 attendees." It caused a shortage of hotel space, cars available for rent, seats on airplanes, etc. It also made the sponsors very happy.

COMDEX had already grown beyond its original intent of being a <u>COM</u>puter <u>D</u>ealers <u>EX</u>hibition. It was already a computer users exhibition that dealers, too, attended.

Observations and notes from the carnival-like show floor:

- The Hot Spots were Windows 3.0 and Notebook computers. Every PC manufacturer had a brand new Notebook to show us.
- Booths showing mainframes were deserted. This was not the right venue for selling big, expensive machines.

- The vendors competed not only in products, but in give-aways. There were souvenirs galore! They were being collected by the shopping bag full. The shopping bags themselves were a popular give-away.
- The most popular booth, by far, was WordPerfect's. They put on a song-and-dance—literally. And they did it every half-hour. There were hats for everybody and prizes for many. Good prizes: laptops and printers.
- The loudest booth, by far, was also WordPerfect's. The audience for the mini-shows were asked to shout, whistle, and stamp their feet. And they did!
- Word Star had a booth, too. They tried to show how poor the WordPerfect product was. They failed.
- Lotus Notes was a new item. It received a lot of attention.
- Microsoft gave out free software.

- **COMDEX**, Fall, 1991

  - The two booths attracting the most attention were WordPerfect and Borland. It wasn't the excellence of their technology, or the magnificence of their product line, it was because they were giving away white hats and T-shirts.

- We estimated that WordPerfect gave away about $100,000 in software packages!
- Hewlett-Packard was trying to sell their new hand-held computer.
- Some of the exhibitors were complaining about price gouging for needed services and about not having access to the show floor for setup time.
- Some booths were forced to be located in outlying hotels. Their draw suffered.
- The hot product this year: Pen-based computers. They didn't seem to work well at all, but everybody wanted to try one.
- A product being shown only by Asian manufacturers: desktop computers with a small footprint.
- The darlings of last year's show, the Notebooks, were taken for granted this year. They generated no excitement, yet some of them were way superior to what was available last year. Shopper, thy name is "fickle!"

- **COMDEX**, Fall, 1992

    The crowds were bigger than ever and the booths were bigger than ever! Some booths were so large they required an army of attendants. They looked like budget-busters!

    - Microsoft was omnipresent! Almost every booth selling software flaunted a yellow sign proclaiming that **this** product worked on Windows. Over 250 Microsoft application packages were on display.
    - IBM had separate booths for each of its product lines. Each booth was manned by IBMers in a different colored polo shirt. All IBMers wore sneakers. (*If everybody wears it, it's still a uniform!*)
    - Times were tougher this year. WordPerfect gave away much less software.
    - 3.5-inch diskettes were a big item. The 5.25-inch diskettes were fading fast. (*Trivia item: They were sitting at a table in a cocktail bar. The one said, "How big should we make the diskette? The other picked up a napkin and said, "How about this size? They both agreed. The napkin was a 5.25 inches square.)*

- Some booths were doing such good business that they were running out of supplies.
- On a few occasions, we stopped at a booth and requested a demonstration only to be told by the attendant, "I don't know how to work it." What were they doing there? Stay home! Save Money!
- Hot product this year: touch screens. They were there in a zillion variations. The quality ranged from poor to amazing!
- Favorite giveaway: a wooden pointer that bore the inscription, "The beatings will continue until morale improves!"

- **COMDEX**, Fall, 1994

  - Biggest one yet! The Microsoft booth alone was bigger than the entire exhibition at some of the small conferences!
  - There were many fewer prizes and giveaways than in previous years.
  - Hot product of the year: CD-ROMs.
  - There were contrasting celebrities decorating two booths. One had Dr. Ruth, the other had a porno queen signing autographs. Dr. Ruth outdrew the porno queen.

- The multimedia booths were grouped together. It became a cacophony of dueling speakers. It seemed each booth would increase the decibels in an effort to be heard over its neighbor. By show's end the attendants must have been hearing-impaired. Some attendees avoided the whole area to avoid the noise.
- Pentax was showing "Pocketjet," a tiny portable printer for use with Notebooks. The print quality was excellent. Drawback: it required special paper.
- Products for the home market were being introduced.
- Attendance exceeded 200, 000 for the first time.

- **COMDEX**, Fall 1995

  - One booth was advertising that they have the **only** pen-based scanner. It can be used to scan words or paragraphs from a book. A little further on, we found another booth advertising a pen-based scanner! We asked, "How can you have one if they say they have the **only** one?" The answer we got was, "They do! They manufacture the hardware and we write software for it. Our software is better than their software."

- At another booth the attendant said, "We have the newest and best handwriting recognition software available today!" He wrote out a sentence and the machine printed it perfectly. My colleague and I asked, "Can we try it?" He said, "This is a demo, we don't want attendees to actually **use** it." (*We were wearing PRESS Badges*.) After much persuasion, he agreed to our request. However, we were told that "this model only recognizes **numbers** if it hasn't been set for your handwriting." "Okay, we will just write numbers." We wrote our telephone number. The machine couldn't read it. "You have to write carefully." "Okay." We wrote carefully. The machine couldn't read it. He said, "Here, let me do it." He carefully wrote our telephone number. The machine couldn't read it.

- Next booth: "Our software translates into six languages. Which would you like to see?" "Italian." He typed in a sentence. The translation was perfect. "Can I try it?" "We aren't supposed to let attendees use the equipment." "Please." "Oh, all right!" We typed in, "All is well!" The machine flunked.

- The CompuServe network went down for a half-hour. CompuServe was embarrassed.
- Sitting through one demo, in the middle of it the screen flashed, "Out of resources." The demo was started over: "Out of resources." End of demo.
- The NetScape booth attracted large crowds.
- Writable CD-drives broke the $1,000 barrier!

- **COMDEX**, Fall 1996

  - Hot product of the year: DVD
  - New product line: accessories for Digital Cameras.
  - Rapidly expanding product line: speech recognition.
  - One attendee, a grade-school teacher, told us that most children entering kindergarten already know how to use a mouse.
  - Product seen in many booths: aids for creating your own Web page.
  - Some game companies were giving away CDs that allowed you to play their game **once**.
  - "Cassiopeia" was attracting attention. It was Casio's tiny hand-held computer. It

had a very large price and a tiny keyboard (*just the right size for Lilliputians*).

- Set-top boxes for attachment to your TV were being introduced.

- **COMDEX**, Fall, 1998
    - There was a general impression that some of the luster was gone. Attendance appeared to be down. There were actually some hotel rooms still available in Las Vegas. (*Albeit at extraordinary prices! During COMDEX, prices jump from three to ten times. It's obscene! Perhaps that is contributing to the declining attendance.*)
    - One area of the show floor was doing a brisk business: the Career Fair.
    - Hottest product line: Anything to do with Voice and/or Speech.
    - Proof that a demo is a demo is a demo: one booth featured a dictation machine. The attendant spoke into the little microphone and the machine printed out the dictation. At one point, the machine started printing **before** the attendant spoke. (*Ooops!*)
    - The booths with Digital Cameras were popular. The picture quality has

improved dramatically, but the prices remained high.

- Language translation machines were also popular. We closely examined two competing products: one expensive, one not. Our test, to the chagrin of the exhibitors, was to ask for a translation from English into Italian for the sentence, "I am well and the well is full of water." (*In Italian, those should be two different words for "well."*) Result: the cheaper product did fine. The expensive product flunked!
- The Fuji Film booth showed a video that was supposed to shock. It was **gross**!

# THE INTERNET

Are there conferences dedicated solely to the Internet? Absolutely! They are easy to find. What is extremely difficult to find is a conference that has **nothing** to do with the Internet!

For this chapter, I will list pertinent comments without noting the source unless the source would help you to interpret the comment. These notes are from about a dozen different conferences:

- The Internet is part hype and part hope.
- The Internet is creating a new market.
- The Internet is borderless commerce.
- There is so much content it's like having 500,000 free channels!
- The trick is to get the value of the content so high that people will be willing to pay for it.
- We are trying to develop Web sites without knowing enough about our customers.
- The Internet isn't business-like. It's anarchy! (*Schussel*)
- The Internet has won! It's **the** data transport system!

- It allows new stuff that was never planned for.
- Half of the home pages are outdated.
- I have to load software and it never loads right! With the Web, I ask for something and I get it!
- You need memory and space to load software, but not on the Internet.
- It' frustrating to wait for graphics!
- An advance in technology can kill a killer application.
- It's much more complex than most people think.
- If you have a successful Web page, you will have millions of people trying to get to it. That's a problem!
- Instead of building user-friendly systems, we have been looking for system friendly users. (*Atre*)
- I don't want information by the ton, I want it by the ounce! (*Steve Mills, IBM*)
- When you demo on the Internet, you need a trouble-shooter with you.
- The content creation tools **stink**!
- Graphics editors require highly skilled operators.
- This is the hottest technology since the invention of the light bulb! (*Wang*)

- We take 20,000 to 30,000 hits a day on our Web page. But, are we making money on it? No, not yet. (*Wang*)
- Don't forget that your competitors will be looking at your Web site, too. It's the biggest activity on the Web! (*Atre*)
- Not having a Web page is like not having a telephone!
- The Internet will be used for customized training.
- The business models always **sound** logical!
- It's a new revenue stream!
- People are sanely and rationally investing in this new business opportunity.
- Anybody can put up a Web page, but can anybody else find it?
- Once you attract them to your site, you have to get them into the habit of returning. It's the key to economic success.
- The Internet can be used for the entire sales cycle and can also foster brand awareness.
- It can be the single point of contact for marketing, sales, and operations.
- The benefits you will accrue include lower cost, increased revenue, and increased corporate efficiencies.

- Your Web site should address the needs of your audience. It requires constant attention because their needs change.
- Everything that appears to be free isn't free.
- The Internet is an even bigger deal than we made it out to be!
- The Internet is the world's largest experiment in anarchy! Can any government stop it?
- We are in a war for eyeballs! We are in competition with television. We need **irresistible** uses! (*Andy Grove, Intel*)
- Dead Web sites frustrate users.
- Andy Grove wants your eyeballs. Bill Gates just wants your money!
- The Internet has allowed us to do things in a better way. (*Gates*)
- A lot of the Web is difficult to use and **boring**.
- Do you want to be a Web-potato?
- The Internet is being held to a higher standard than the rest of the world.
- Branding on the Internet is difficult. It takes longer.
- Certain Web sites are joyful to use. Others are a pain in the neck!
- On the Internet, you can sell anything that someone wants to buy!

- Among the best business uses of the Internet are gathering competitive information, providing customer service, acquiring customer feedback, and distributing information.
- You need an Internet Evangelist. Without one, the budget issues get hairy!
- The big cost savings come from changing printed materials to on-line and providing on-line training with Web-based materials.
- Sell advertising!
- You can sell all around the world!
- Give them an on-line demo free. If they like it, they buy it!
- Give away free samples. To send it to them you need their name and address!
- Mobile communications can ruin a vacation!
- Online services will change education.
- Our eighth grade students know more about computers than the superintendent of schools.
- We think the Internet represents the most powerful representation of networking. (*Gerstner, IBM*)
- There is a gold rush to the Internet, but there really is gold there! (*Gates*)

- There is talk of a TV with 500 channels. With the Internet, you get only one channel, but you control what's on it!
- The Internet allows people to realize there is a global community. For kids, that's great!
- The Web is not just another form of print.
- Nobody in business browses. We **hunt**!
- Don't put obstacles in the users path.
- Masses of content will not grab an audience.
- You have to provide ease of navigation and make it **fun** to use!
- Brain-dumping is boring!
- Poor design can be disastrous!
- Just because you **can** do it doesn't mean you **should** do it!
- Forgetting to close the sale is **stupid**!
- A good Web application has a clear purpose.
- Go for simplicity!
- When you set up a Web site, remember that not everybody has fancy equipment. Keep it simple!
- A Web site needs a complete intolerance for downtime. Have a robot check your site **constantly**.
- Make the page **interesting**, not a technology marvel!

- A promotional Web site used to be adequate. Now, you need sales, service, support, etc.
- It requires increasing sophistication.
- Identify your users, understand their behavior, and reach out to them **individually**.
- Who owns the content on your site?
- A poor site can drive customers away.
- Be careful! There are advertising regulations.
- Don't infringe on copyrights, trademarks, etc.
- A virus can cause costly damage.
- Software can damage **other** software.
- Your contract should specify jurisdiction and the limits of liability.
- Bottom line: no security, no business!
- Every modem is a potential problem.
- You can't leave security to the end-user.
- There is never 100% security. Somebody is always coming up with something new!
- The Internet was not designed to be secure. The designers never thought that **millions** of people would be online!
- The Internet was designed to be **reliable** and **available**.

- Unsophisticated people can get their hands on sophisticated tools. They do damage.
- There are two types of security: very good and none at all!
- I don't want fancy graphics on my site because I don't want people to wait. (*Carpenter, IBM*)
- There will always be scarce resources on the Internet.
- Always have a backup server running!
- How do you connect the Internet together? By ad hoc arrangements. (*Malamud*)
- The Internet is messy! It's too huge for strict order to be imposed. (*Malamud*)
- It was the relaxation of government regulations the allowed commercial users to join the Internet. (*Cerf*)
- Scientists are using the Internet to link laboratories around the world. Name of the network: Collaboratory. (*Cerf*)
- The Internet is effecting changes in time and space, society, expression, politics, education, economics, perception, and reality. It is effecting our lives!
- It is an invaluable tool for enhancing productivity.
- If you are waiting for something to **replace** the Internet, forget it!

- The Internet is growing faster than a cancer!
- On the Web, there is a clear distinction between bad design and bad content.
- People expect Web sites to look the way they work and work the way they look.
- All the principles of design and usability that apply elsewhere also apply to the Web.
- The content should be interesting and valuable, but not overwhelming.
- Give people a meaningful reason to return.
- Use just the right amount of technology to deliver the message.
- It takes time to learn how to do Web design.
- Test! Use beta tests!
- Every little detail in a user interface is important.
- Users can notice details on a subconscious level and they will be affected—positively or negatively. It will affect the user's confidence in the site and the material on display.
- Provide the features and functions the users want and need.
- The use must be obvious or at least discoverable.

- The users should be productive. They should achieve their goals and enjoy doing it.
- Your site should be content-centric.
- Your site is an extension of your corporate image. It needs to look and feel like the rest of your company.
- Don't create a bunch of disconnected pages devoid of relationships.
- You need both: **consistency and continuity**.
- The larger your site, the greater your need for consistency and continuity.
- Do a reality check. Is your message being conveyed?
- Don't give the user "artsy-fartsy"!
- Don't rename a page after the links have been established.
- Make sure your site is readable. Pay attention to color, font patterns and texture as well as contrast between background and foreground.
- Aesthetics are important! First impressions **do** count!
- Users don't like to scroll.
- Avoid text-only pages.
- Be sure your pages are printable.
- Offend no one. Beware of cultural differences.

- Don't make assumptions, but do challenge assumptions.
- Examine your site. Be a nitpicker!
- You can't use the Web for business unless you keep it up at all times.
- There are issues that are non-technical and non-commercial. Examples censorship, free speech, cryptography, and copyrights. (*Dyson*)
- Creativity will flourish if the creators are paid for their work. Artists have to eat, too!
- The Internet raises some new legal problems.
- On the Internet, the **small** guys can compete with the **big** guys.
- It's a storefront for worldwide products.
- Fun sites are the ones that attract attention.
- You can give previews of software over the Internet.
- The Internet can cover areas where there are no retailers.
- The Internet has a problem we should be happy to have: rapid growth!
- The Internet is extending the business horizon.
- Use the Internet to inspire a love of learning in children. Then, the love becomes an addiction.

- The Internet can be used as an individual tutor that works at the level of the individual child.
- With the Internet, we can teach 50 million kids at the same time!
- Nobody knows how much money is being made on the Internet.
- The negative comments about the Internet are far outweighed by the benefits.
- The whole household uses the Net.
- The Internet is a new medium, don't use it the same way you used the old media. (*Barksdale, Netscape*)
- The Internet is akin to the Wild West meets cyberspace!
- Just because something is old doesn't mean it's not copyrighted.
- It's not the number of hits on your site that's important, it's the **consequence** of those hits!
- When they click the mouse to your Web site you have their complete attention. Cash in on it immediately! (*Negroponte*)
- The Internet is not free. You just pay for it in a different way. (*Negroponte*)
- The Web is click-and-wait. (*Lucky*)
- There is no centralized Internet strategy.
- We can delegate responsibility, but we can't abdicate it!

- Don't build expectations you can't fulfill.
- The Internet will seed some of the major companies of the next century.
- The people it will influence most are our grandchildren.
- It provides easy access to the global market.
- The Web is a lonely place. It lacks a social experience. (*Not any more! Now, it can sometimes get too personal!*)
- Chat is popular if somewhat vacuous.
- The new media is confronting old attitudes.
- The Internet is the democratization of computing. (*Atre*)
- The marriage of the Internet and data warehousing is a killer application.
- The Web should be just one piece of your marketing mix.
- You get immediate feedback from the Web. That helps Marketing.
- Learn which messages are motivating visits and which messages capture the most attention.
- Calculate the cost-per-lead and coast-per-sale using the Internet.
- Produce reports to analyze your advertising investment in the Internet.

- The Internet was designed for public access. Therefore, it is inherently insecure.
- Using the Internet, you can have one-on-one relations with **thousands** of your customers.
- Test your design. Find the people that complain the most and ask **them** to be testers.
- All user actions should have an immediate feedback.
- Be helpful and polite when reporting a user error. Show how the error can be corrected.
- Icons should be intuitively and immediately understood.
- If you look at a page and don't immediately know what's going on, something is wrong!
- Be lenient with user formats: accept "5" instead of "05."
- Too many frames cause confusion.
- Leave some white space.
- The user is **always** right!
- If the users are all making the same mistake, the package wasn't designed right.
- Anticipate mistakes and make them easy to correct.
- Don't jam everything onto one page.

- The Internet is beyond a technology revolution, it's a **social** revolution!
- It's a tool for both mass and direct marketing.
- It will be as important and as critical as the telephone system was.
- Look for ways to exploit the Web.
- Don't have the technical staff design your Web page. (*Good advice!*)
- A lousy market plan looks even worse when you put it on the Internet!
- It's not the technology, it's the **content** that gets people to buy!
- It's only as good as the users say it is. **Their** opinion counts, not yours.
- On the Internet, there is no coordination, but there is no monopoly either. (*Cerf*)
- You can reach people anywhere in the world **instantly**. That is **power**!
- The most sophisticated network means nothing to people who aren't connected to it. (*Hundt, FGG Chairman*)

Lots of people have lots of things to say about the Internet.  What they still don't have is a uniform opinion (*beyond **it's wonderful**)!*

# ELECTRONIC COMMERCE

Is Electronic Commerce (EC) changing the way the world does business? Oh, Yeah! Verily!

Is EC a popular topic at conferences? Silly question!

First we will examine some conferences where EC was a major focus:

- **The Business OnLine Symposium** (Giga Information Group, 1996, San Francisco)

    The opening presentation was delivered by two speakers: Gay Slesinger (Giga) and Mike Taylor (Arthur D. Little).

    "EC encompasses more than just the transactions between a business and its customers. It also includes the transactions between that business and its suppliers, partners, banks, etc. The information flow can be bi-directional among suppliers, manufacturers, distributors, retailers and buyers."

    "Every experiment into EC has not been a huge success. There are barriers to its success. Some barriers are technical (security, lack of standards, etc.) some are behavioral (shopping patterns, lack of expert salesperson interaction, etc.) and a few are institutional (legal complications, payment infrastructure, etc.)." The speakers quickly pointed out that "the barriers are falling away."

They listed the "driving forces" behind EC:
  direct buying relationships
  cost reduction
  unlimited shelf space
  geographic reach
  market share expansion
  customer share expansion

The **buyer**'s drives are somewhat different:
  information access
  convenience
  depth
  buyer control
  time savings
  cost savings
  wider selection

They said that some aspects of EC should be inter-linked. Their list of those:
  public relations and advertising
  marketing
  selling

fulfilling and delivering
servicing
getting paid

Other technologies that can be built into
your EC system include:
imaging
bar coding
computer enabled FAX
point-of-sale equipment
computer telephony
workflow systems
electronic forms

At the time, I suggested that a few more
items should be added to that last list:
data warehousing
data analysis and reporting
automated business rules

The speakers warned us that the hype about
EC isn't always correct. They presented a
long list of examples. Here, for your
edification, are a few samples of the
examples:

Hype: Be there first!
Reality: Do it well!

Hype: A Web site means free advertising!
Reality: It's expensive!

Hype: You reach a mass market!
Reality: It's a self-segmented consumer market!

Hype: Success is determined by the number of hits!
Reality: Success is determined by the conversion rate! (*Results!*)

Hype: The data is timely!
Reality: Only if someone updates it!

Hype: We are dealing with mass scale!
Reality: You should be looking at customization!

Hype: Always use online delivery!
Reality: For a refrigerator?

Hype: Offer immediate gratification!
Reality: How about **rapid** gratification?

Hype: Get rich quick!
Reality: Be prepared to spend a lot!

Hype: You have to rely on credit cards!
Reality: No you don't! There are different payment methods.

Hype: It's impersonal. You broadcast!
Reality: It should be personal and interactive!

They warned that your EC strategy must fit in with your corporate strategy.

"EC is resulting in a revolution for marketing, sales, and support." It can offer new distribution channels, new products and services, and result in a stronger, tighter value chain." And, its use is not restricted to corporate giants. Even small companies can take advantage of its benefits.

- **The Business OnLine Symposium** (Giga Information Group, 1997, San Francisco)

  The final speaker at this conference was Jim Johnson, head of the United States delegation to the G8 Electronic Commerce Policy Group. My notes from his presentation include:

"The United States has resolved that the private sector should be in the leadership position for EC."

He warned that some countries see the Internet as "an American tool for economic conquest."

"The I/T industry has not been government regulated. They want to keep the government out of the industry and they want the government to 'go away.' The fact is that the government **will not** go away!"

"EC will impact the **government** as well as business and the way we live."

"We learned that no government in the world is organized to handle EC."

"Every country in the world is doing something about EC."

"EC needs a harmonization of accounting standards."

"The issue of taxes on the Internet is wide open and **very** controversial."

"In the United States, State governments are getting involved in EC. The result is a lack of coordination and conformity."

"The Federal Trade Commission is looking into the effect of the Internet on children."

Here are a collection of notes taken at a variety of conferences:

- Over optimism and over pessimism are both associated with EC.
- Virtual malls are a **ridiculous** model!
- Some of the predictions are out-and-out-**wrong**!
- Advertising on the Web **works**!
- Our software creates a personalized sales assistant.
- We have to offer services they **can't** get over the telephone.
- EC is the **best** direct marketing device that ever was!
- There are incredible opportunities for providing one-on-one service.
- EC is a serious market!
- All the money you save in procurement goes directly into your bottom line!
- Make it easy for the customer to do business with you.

- EC looks deceptively, seductively simple. It's really complex!
- EC is a vision for global trading communities.
- EC revolutionizes the business!
- You can use EC to expand the number of your suppliers.
- EC is not a new market, it's an evolution of commerce!
- In EC, there are so many choices that it's as bad as having no choice!
- The goals of EC are the same as the goals of regular commerce. The difference is that a new means to those goals is now available.
- There is a long way to go before EC replaces regular commerce!
- We have been doing elements of EC for years!
- EC doesn't have to be cosmic! Relatively simple transactions can be very helpful.
- For EC, the Web sites are overwhelmingly in the US, overwhelmingly in English, and the transactions are overwhelmingly in dollars.
- Electronic **Business** is more than EC, it covers all kinds of electronic interaction: order fulfillment, customer service, retrieving information, etc.
- EC involves running a virtual company.

- The traditional market leaders are being threatened. I/T has become a strategic weapon!
- Don't expect to get large revenues right away.
- The first advantage will be cutting cost, the next will be reaching new customers.
- Customer service is a differentiator.
- It's not enough to just have a Web site. You have to provide for a **complete** business.
- Transform your Web site into a sophisticated EC system integrated with existing order processing, fulfillment, logistics, customer service, and inventory management applications.
- If you go to EC, you have to be concerned about the level of network service you need and get.
- The consumer's concerns are price and convenience.
- Word-of-mouth is what leads people to a site.
- E-mail and links to other sites are performing better than banners.
- English is the default language, but leverage local languages.
- The problem with EC is not the "E" it's the "C"!

- Everybody is rushing to EC but we have a Tower of Babel problem! There is no common **business** language!
- The biggest hurdle is getting the customer to buy the **first** time.
- If you maintain a relationship with your customers they become your sales force!
- When they ask a question, they will come back for the answer.
- Get the profiles of your customers so you can send them useful information and offer them useful products.
- Reach out to your customers **individually**.
- Selling on the Internet takes discipline and commitment. It's hard work and it costs money!
- It's possible to do it right the first time, but a lot of that is luck!
- If it's on the Internet, it's **automatically** global!
- If you don't know the laws in Germany or Japan, you may be violating them.
- A major factor will be micro-transactions. If you have several million of them, it turns out to be big business.
- Don't look at the excitement, look at the consequences!

Does EC have any potential for you? The probable answer is "Probably."

# <u>CONCLUSIONS</u>

Comparatively speaking, the waters are now calm.
The feeding frenzy is over.   The turmoil and
roiling waters have calmed down - at least on the
surface. What is happening below the surface is
not visible to the buying public. Is it kinda like a
duck swimming?

When you think about it, selling I/T-Ware is not
only more fun, it is also easier than selling a lot of
other things. You can give sexy demonstrations,
the people you are trying to impress are **really**
interested in technology, you've **always** got
something new to sell, and, if the prices are
moving at all, they are coming **down**! You have it
made! There are just a few things you should
remember:

- Make sure your product is salable. Test it
  yourself! Test it as the **user** will be using
  it. Are you satisfied? If you are satisfied,
  there is a pretty good chance the other
  users will be, too. However, if you
  **aren't** satisfied, …
- Don't try to push **anything** on a
  customer (*or they may push back*).
  Allow them to convince **themselves** that
  they want and need your product. Let

them sell **themselves**. You be their source of information and their guide to the rewards we all know they will accrue. As Woody Allen asked in one of his movies, "Who are you going to believe, me or you?" Get them to believe themselves.

- Know your competition. Know their strengths and their weaknesses. Never provide them with ammunition they can use against you.

- Feel secure with your security. Investigate. If there are any exposures, make sure they get plugged. Even a small breach of security can hurt you a lot!

- Support your Support Services and make sure they are supporting **you**. They can be a great source of customer information. Listen to what they can tell you.

- Use your User Groups. (*If such there be.*) A User Group meeting is a **marvelous** place to meet and greet your customers. Listen to their dreams and aspirations (*and complaints*). See how you can make their life more pleasant. They will appreciate it. That will work to **your** benefit.

- There are **hundreds** of I/T conferences each year. Be aware of the different types and know how you can use **each** to your advantage. Each and every one of these conferences is a gathering place for hundreds or thousands of people who have traveled distances, spent money, and invested time because they are interested in **I/T-Ware**! What a wonderful opportunity for you! Act!

- The Internet exists! Use it! Be innovative! Use it **better** and more **profitably** than your competition is doing.
- How is Electronic Commerce affecting you? What else **could** you be doing with it? What else **should** you be doing with it? *(Those are two very different questions*!)

The two companies I mentioned most were IBM and Univac. Having worked for both of them, I was able to observe their marketing/sales tactics and the consequences of those tactics. Basically, IBM built products to please their **customers** and Univac built products that pleased their own **engineers**. In some cases and in some ways, the Univac product was technically superior, but so what? Beta was technically superior to VHS, too. Again, so what? Build it so that they **want** to come can be a much better tactic than build it and wait for them to come.

Go forth and try some new avenues to success. You won't know which one works best for you until you have tried them all. Do something different!

One final thing: Even in a feeding frenzy, you have to be using the right bait! Cheese and peanut butter may work great to catch a mouse (*even if you don't have that super trap we designed*) but it won't help you to catch a shark or any other fish. Alter your sales pitch to fit your audience and the current situation. The CEO will probably have slightly different interests and goals from the CFO and the CIO will definitely have different interests and goals from most of the troops reporting to him/her.

Oh, another "final thing." When you try to help you customer, make sure you really are helping them. The other day we received a large package in the mail. I had the devil of a time figuring how to open it. After an unpleasant struggle I did manage to get it open. Inside the box, right on top where they thought it would be convenient, were detailed instructions on how to open the box. Thanks a lot!